To Bob,
and all who share
their life and love through cooking.

Food Processor Cookbook

A special edition of Nitty Gritty Productions' Food Processor Cookbook.

by
Janis Wicks

Illustrated by Mike Nelson

A Nitty Gritty Book*
Published by
Nitty Gritty Productions
P.O. Box 5457
Concord, California 94524

*Nitty Gritty Books—Trademark
Owned by Nitty Gritty Productions
Concord, California

ISBN 0-911954-41-4

Table of Contents

Introduction 1

Getting Acquainted 7

Blending • Slicing • Shredding • Chopping • Puréing 33

Cookies and Pastry 89

Pâte à Choux 105

Puff Paste 117

Yeast Breads and Rolls 127

Cakes and Quick Breads 143

Creative Returns 155

New Horizons 165

Index 180

Introduction

Loving to cook lead me to study home economics, and to a husband who likes to eat and travel. Pursuing our interests—now expanded into food, wine and travel—I found myself studying at Cordon Bleu in Paris, and then teaching French cooking in my home. Now, for nine years I've shared inspiration and recipes with friends and students in the San Francisco Bay area, and with my own four children.

In our kitchen we all use the food processor. What a timesaver! We find it fun to use and easy to clean up, with time left over for more cooking and writing this cookbook. It is my desire that this book will bring pleasure to all cooks who own a food processor.

I have set the book up as a series of learning procedures or mini-lessons, arranged in order of difficulty from easiest to most involved. It is hoped that the procedures presented in the recipes will be applied to others in your own collection. For those who have already had experience with a food processor, I hope you will find new ideas and recipes which will soon take their place among your favorites.

The Getting Acquainted section includes recipes using each of the blades for rather simple tasks. To obtain the maximum benefit of owning a food processor, you must put it to use for even the most ordinary kitchen tasks. In the beginning you may have to train yourself to look for steps in a recipe which the processor can do. Soon you will do this automatically. When there is a job to be done, if it's feasable, let the food processor do it! It blends, slices, shreds, chops and purees beautifully. The "mess" is contained making the clean up simple. Using the food processor efficiently reduces the difficulty of many preparations, and helps you speed through time consuming tasks. This allows for more fun in cooking, less time spent in clean up and energy leftover to enjoy the results.

Keep in mind, the food processor handles small quantities (baby food for one serving, filling for one sandwich or a little pâté from the remains of last night's dinner) just as well as large amounts. A pound or two of mushrooms for duxelles used to take an hour to finely chop and clean up the mess. Now it takes five minutes. And, I'm sure you have the memory of a really good onion soup, but the thought of slicing six or eight large onions may have kept you from preparing it. Put it off no longer! With your food processor and the recipe on page 18 you can easily satisfy your longing, and there are no tears when the processor does the slicing.

From Getting Acquainted, the book continues on to family favorites which are grouped together according to the blade or disc they require. There are sections on pastry making, yeast breads and rolls, quick puff paste, and pâte à choux (cream puff paste), which is made unbelievably fast and perfectly with a food processor. And how versatile it is. A Swiss cheese ring to serve with wine, potato gnocchi and heavenly small puffs filled with French pastry cream and topped with chocolate sauce ... all made from the basic pâte à choux. Still to follow are sections on cakes and quick breads, innovations with leftovers and the exciting New Horizons section.

With a food processor in your kitchen you are led to new adventures in cooking. Things you would have rejected ... too much work, too messy, too many steps in preparation, too much clean up ... no longer fit into these catagories. I encourage you to consider some of the more advanced preparations in the New Horizons section. These recipes fall into the classification of "haute cuisine." They are more involved but not necessarily more difficult. Many require advance preparation, and some can be assembled as much as 24 hours ahead, if desired, enabling you to relax and enjoy your "masterpieces" along with your guests.

Using a food processor is easy ... the same applies to the clean up. What more could one ask? A dishwashing brush with a long handle is a must for cleaning the discs and blades. They are sharp and fingers are best kept out of the way. I also use a small round brush (the kind used to clean coffeepot stems) to clean the core of the steel blade when necessary.

If you haven't already done so, make a permanent place on the counter for your food processor. You won't want to get it out of a cupboard as many times as you can think to use it. Keep blade and discs safely stored nearby where they are easy to reach. Special plastic holders are available and magnetic knife holders work for the steel blade and discs. Or, place them in a drawer in such a way they can't slide around. I fit the discs flat against the side of the drawer with towels next to them to hold them up. Give it a little thought and you'll find an ideal place.

I hope you will enjoy this book and find it useful. I know you will enjoy your food processor and use it often.   Janis Wicks
Walnut Creek, California

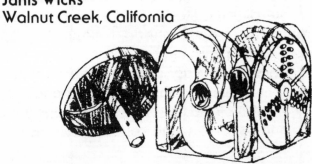

About White Pepper, Nutmeg,
Bouquet Garni And Lemon Zest

I call for <u>freshly ground white pepper</u> and <u>freshly grated nutmeg</u> together in many recipes, having been influenced by my experience with French cooking where they are added to all cream and butter sauces, egg dishes and pâte à choux. They are usually used in equal amounts (1/8 teaspoon), but let your own taste be your guide. Freshly grated white pepper is more subtle than black and I prefer it. White peppercorns and whole nutmeg can be found in markets in the Spice Islands rack, or in spice and import shops. All is lost when they are pre-ground, and they contribute little by comparison. A light colored grinder is handy for white peppercorns and a small nutmeg grater costs less than a dollar. I keep both handy to my cooking area.

<u>To make a bouquet garni</u>, begin with a 3 to 4-inch rib of celery. Lay 3 to 4 sprigs fresh thyme (1/4 to 1/2 teaspoon dried) in celery depression. Lay 1 small bay leaf over thyme. Double the stems of 3 to 4 sprigs parsley back and forth to hold everything together. Lay on top of bay leaf. Tie with string, winding diagonally down celery and back. After using bouquet garni, lift out with a fork. Place in a sieve and press with the back of a spoon to extract juices and rich flavors. Discard.

<u>Lemon zest</u> is the colored part of the lemon peel only . . . without any of the white flesh. It is easily removed with a vegetable peeler.

5

Getting Acquainted

If you are the new owner of a food processor, practice turning it "on" and "off" . . . without blades. This helps to get the "feel" of starting and stopping. Then try it with the blades in place, and observe how fast they move. Learn to think about turning "off" before turning "on," and be in control. With an appliance that does tasks so quickly, there are times when an almost instant "off" will prevent over-processing.

Next, slice some zucchini or a cucumber. Chop an onion or shred a piece of cheese. What fun! Practice slicing potatoes (and then make scalloped potatoes, page 47) or apples for an apple crisp (page 48). Apples are so thinly and evenly sliced the skins need not be removed. Flour, sugar, oatmeal and butter for the topping can be mixed so quickly, you will have dessert almost prepared and you've just been "playing."

When using your food processor, plan the steps of a recipe with the processor in mind. Maybe the first thing chopped or sliced won't be needed right away, but it's more practical to chop nuts and process dry mixtures before the bowl is used for wet ingredients. With a little advance planning, it usually is not necessary to wash the bowl and blades between operations.

Kneaded Butter

Kneaded butter is made in a food processor in a split second and is a perfect introduction to easier, faster and better cooking made possible by this splendid piece of equipment. Store kneaded butter in the refrigerator and use it for thickening soups or pan juices remaining after braising and roasting. It blends right in without lumping.

1 cup margarine or butter
1-1/4 cups all-purpose flour

Insert **steel blade** in processor bowl. Add butter and process to soften. Add flour and process a few seconds to blend. Turn out onto waxed paper or foil. Shape into an 8-inch-long roll. Wrap tightly and refrigerate. Cut off slices when needed for thickening. Two 1/4-inch-thick slices will thicken one cup liquid to medium consistency. Simmer a few minutes after adding kneaded butter to eliminate the raw taste of flour.

Mornay Sauce

The classic sauce made with Gruyère cheese that has a million uses.

3 ozs. Gruyère cheese
3 cups milk
5 or 6 1/4-inch slices kneaded butter, page 8
<u>or</u> 4 tbs. (1/2 cube) butter and 1/3 cup flour

3/4 tsp. salt
1/8 tsp. freshly ground white pepper
1/8 tsp. freshly grated nutmeg

With **steel blade** inserted in processor bowl, process cheese until finely chopped. Set aside. Heat milk to boiling in a heavy saucepan. Whisk in pieces of kneaded butter until a medium thickness is achieved. (If using butter and flour instead of kneaded butter, melt butter in saucepan. Add flour and cook, stirring, over medium heat for 2 minutes. Whisk in boiling milk.) Add salt, pepper and nutmeg. Cover and let sauce cook very slowly over lowest heat (or transfer to a double boiler) 20 to 30 minutes. Stir occasionally, and clean sides of pan with rubber scraper each time you stir. Add cheese to sauce just before serving. Makes 3 cups.

Duxelles

Duxelles is a kind of mushroom hash whose name you may not recognize. Widely used in French cooking, its concentrated flavor makes it an ideal seasoning for sauces and stuffings and as a garnish ingredient. Finely chopping mushrooms for duxelles, by hand, is a time-consuming chore. With a food processor it is an enjoyable procedure, accomplished in seconds. Duxelles is a mixture you will use in many ways now that it is so easily made.

1/2 lb. mushrooms
2 to 3 shallots, 1/2 med. onion or
    4 to 5 green onion blubs
1-1/2 tbs. butter
1-1/2 tbs. oil
1/2 tsp. salt
1/4 tsp. pepper
1 to 2 tbs. Madeira or sherry wine

With **steel blade** inserted place half of mushrooms in processor bowl. If mushrooms are large break them with your fingers as you drop them into the bowl. Cover bowl and process until finely chopped, but not pulverized. Turn the processor "on-off" to check the size of the mushroom pieces. Transfer chopped mushrooms to a bowl. Process remaining mushrooms in the same manner. Transfer to bowl and process shallots until minced. Heat butter and oil in a large skillet until very hot and butter is just beginning to brown. Add mushrooms and shallots. Cook, stirring, over medium-high heat until moisture ceases to rise from pan. Mushrooms should not brown, although their color darkens as they cook. Add salt, pepper and wine. If not using duxelles right away, cool and pack into covered containers. Store in refrigerator up to five days or in freezer for several months. Makes about 2/3 cup duxelles.

Stuffed Eggs Mornay

The stuffing is made with duxelles, the flavorful mushroom mixture that makes this dish extra special. Serve at brunch, for a luncheon, as a first course at dinner, or for a late evening supper.

Duxelles, page 10
Mornay Sauce, page 9
12 eggs at room temperature
1/2 tsp. salt
1/8 tsp. white pepper
3 tbs. grated Parmesan or Gruyère cheese
1 tbs. melted butter

Prepare duxelles and Mornay sauce well in advance of use, if desired. Hard cook eggs*. While still warm, cut eggs in half lengthwise. Remove yolks and drop into processor bowl fitted with the **steel blade.** Add salt and pepper. Process until smooth. Add 1/3 cup duxelles and enough Mornay sauce to moisten stuffing. Process a few seconds. Place a rounded teaspoonful of stuffing on each of 12 egg halves. Cover with remaining halves. Press each egg together while gently cupping it between your hands. Lightly butter a shallow ovenproof au gratin dish (or individual au gratin or souf-fle dishes or scallop shells). Spread a thin layer of sauce in dish. Arrange stuffed eggs on top. Spoon remaining sauce over eggs, covering them completely. Sprinkle with grated cheese and melted butter. (Dish may be refrigerated at this point.) Heat in 375°F oven about 15 minutes, or until sauce bubbles. Place under broiler briefly to brown cheese. (If assembled ahead and refrigerated, reheat in 350°F oven about 40 minutes, or until bubbly.) Makes 12 first course or 6 luncheon, brunch or buffet servings.

*Hard cook eggs by lowering them with a spoon into boiling water. Adjust the heat to low and simmer 14 minutes. Cool immediately in cold running water. Drain, and shake eggs in pan to crack shells. Peel and dry on paper toweling.

Spanish Peanut Butter

For a change in flavor and texture, process Spanish peanuts. Rub lightly in a clean dish towel to remove some of the salt and some skins. (No need to remove all skins.) Using the **steel blade,** process 1-1/2 to 2 cups peanuts at a time until smooth and an oily texture develops. Store in covered container in the refrigerator.

Almonds and cashews can be treated in the same manner.

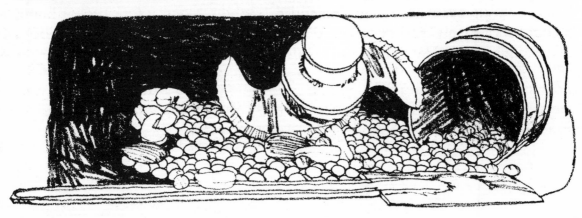

Chopping and Shredding Cheese

FIRM CHEESE (steel blade)

Firm cheeses, such as Parmesan, natural Gruyère, imported Swiss, aged Cheddar, Kasseri, Fontinella, etc., are actually chopped, rather than grated.

Remove any skin or hard rinds from cheese. With a large knife, firm hand and cutting board, divide cheese into 1/2-inch portions. With **steel blade** inserted in bowl, start processor. Drop pieces of cheese through feed tube, and process (chop) until desired fineness is achieved. If you notice unusual thumping, stop processor immediately. Check for too firm pieces of cheese caught on edge of blade. Loosen pieces from blade and continue processing.

SOFT CHEESE (shredding disc)

Soft cheeses, such as Monterey Jack, Finnish Lappi, Mozzarella, mild Cheddar, etc., shred beautifully in a matter of seconds.

Cut cheese into pieces about 1 x 2 x 3-inches, which will fit into the feed tube. Insert **shredding disc** in bowl, and stand pieces of cheese in feed tube. Use the pusher and moderate pressure. If processor vibrates excessively, stop it immediately. Perhaps the cheese is firmer than you judged. In that case, switch to the **steel blade,** and process as for firm cheese.

15

Cheese Souffle

A wonderful spur-of-the-moment dish, ready to serve in 20 minutes. Souffles are fun to make, and I've never found anyone who doesn't enjoy watching one being put together.

2 oz. Gruyère, Tybo, or other flavorful cheese
4 tbs. butter
1 cup milk
3 tbs. flour
1/2 tsp. salt
1/8 tsp. white pepper
1/8 tsp. grated nutmeg
3 egg yolks
4 egg whites

With **shredding disc** or **steel blade** inserted (depending on whether cheese is soft or firm), process cheese to make 3/4 cup (not packed). Butter a 1 or 1-1/2-quart souffle dish heavily, using 1 tablespoon butter. Set aside. Heat milk to boiling. Melt remaining 3 tablespoons butter in heavy saucepan. Stir in flour. Cook 2 minutes without browning. Remove from heat. Whisk in boiling milk. Add salt, pepper, and nutmeg. Boil at least 3 minutes. Slip egg yolks into sauce, and whisk immediately. Cook one minute longer. Set aside in warm place. Whip egg whites (preferably in a copper bowl with a large whisk) until stiff, but not dry. Stir about one fourth of egg whites into warm sauce to lighten it. Quickly fold sauce into remaining egg whites. Sprinkle on cheese. Fold only until barely blended. Turn into buttered souffle dish, and smooth top with spatula. Clean edge of dish, so no souffle mixture extends over edge. (Souffle may wait half an hour at this point, if necessary. Invert a large pot or bowl over it). Bake in lower third of preheated 475°F oven, with no rack above it, for about 8 minutes, until puffed and lightly browned on top. At this point, turn dish around 180° in oven. Reduce temperature to 425°F for an additional 7 or 8 minutes. Souffle should have risen about 2 inches above dish, and sides will look and feel fairly firm. Center of souffle may be slightly soft, which is preferable. However, for a fimer center, add a few minutes to the last baking time.

French Onion Soup with Croutons

It's worth having a food processor just to make this delicious soup. Imagine slicing onions without tears!

6 large onions, peeled
3 tbs. _each_ butter and oil*
1/3 cup flour
8 cups beef or chicken broth, heated
1 large clove garlic

1 bouquet garni, page 5
freshly ground pepper
1/3 cup dry sherry
2 to 3 tbs. brandy
French Croutons, page 19

Cut onions in half. With **slicing disc** inserted, place cover on processor bowl. Add onions through the feed tube until all are sliced. Heat butter and oil in a large (at least 3 quarts) heavy saucepan. Add sliced onions to hot fat. Cook slowly about 40 minutes, stirring every five or ten minutes. Allow onions to brown slowly, but not burn. Sprinkle flour over onions. Stir until flour is no longer visible. Add hot broth. Continue stirring to loosen all particles from pan. Add minced garlic and bouquet garni. Adjust heat so soup simmers gently. Cook about one hour. Add a little pepper, dry sherry and brandy.

Add salt, if needed. Serve very hot with French Croutons placed in each bowl before ladling in soup.

FRENCH CROUTONS

1-1/2 ozs. (about) Gruyère cheese
6 slices French bread
1 tbs. olive oil

Using **shredding disc,** process cheese. You will have about 1/3 cup when shredding. Distribute over bread slices. Drizzle with olive oil. Heat in 375°F oven until bread is lightly browned and cheese is melted.

*or 1/2 cup chopped fresh pork fat (Use **steel blade** to chop it.)

Making Crumbs and Crumb Crusts

BREAD CRUMBS

Soft—Best made with bread that is a few days old. Tear slices into quarters. Up to four slices can be processed at one time. Use **steel blade.** Place pieces of bread in processor bowl or add through feed tube. Process a few seconds. Store fresh bread crumbs in freezer if not using immediately.

Parsleyed Soft Crumbs—Chop fresh parsley along with pieces of bread.

Buttered Soft Crumbs—Tear bread in quarters. Process using **steel blade.** Add 1 tablespoon butter for each slice of bread. Process until mixed with crumbs.

Dry—Bread must be thoroughly dry. If not, place in 150°F oven for 2 hours. Cut dry bread in 1-inch cubes or chunks. Place two or three handfuls in processor bowl with **steel blade.** Process to desired fineness. If a partially dried piece of bread becomes lodged under blade, stop immediately. Remove blade and turn crumbs out onto waxed paper. Remove and discard troublesome piece. Return blade and crumbs to bowl and continue processing. Dry crumbs can be stored at room temperature for a month or two.

COOKIE CRUMBS

Graham crackers, zweiback, vanilla wafers or other cookies can be reduced to crumbs quickly and easily using the **steel blade.** One-third pound, or about two cups, can be processed at one time. A combination of crumbs is good, and it's an excellent way to use the last of the cookies and the broken crackers in the bottom of the box. Almonds, filberts and walnuts add interesting flavors when a few are processed along with the crumbs.

CRUMB CRUSTS

A little brown or white sugar (amount depends on sweetness of cookies), a dash of cinnamon and 2 to 3 tablespoons butter per cup of crumbs can be added while crumbs are being made.

Broiled Tomatoes

Instant glamour for any meal. A favorite with broiled or barbecued meats or fish.

1 small clove garlic
2 slices stale bread, torn in quarters
2 to 3 sprigs parsley or basil leaves

1 tbs. grated parmesan cheese, optional
salt and freshly ground pepper
1 tbs. butter or olive oil

Insert **steel blade** in food processor. Peel garlic and cut in 2 or 3 pieces. With blades whirling, drop in garlic through feed tube. Add pieces of bread and parsley to processor bowl. Process a few seconds, chopping bread and parsley at the same time. Add parmesan, if desired. Wash tomatoes and cut each in half horizontally. Arrange cut side up in pie plate, au gratin dish or shallow baking pan. Sprinkle with salt and pepper. Scatter crumbs over cut surfaces. Dot with butter or dribble olive oil over crumbs. Bake in 400°F oven 12 to 15 minutes, or broil, 6 inches from heat, until crumbs are lightly browned. Turn off heat. Let sit in oven a few minutes before serving. Makes 6 servings.

French Cheese Cake

Make in an 8-inch springform pan. Lining the bottom with baking parchment allows you to slip the cheese cake off the metal base for more gracious serving.

CRUSTS
2-1/2 tbs. butter
1 cup fine zweibach or other crumbs (see page 22)
1 tbs. sugar
1/4 tsp. cinnamon

Coat sides of springform with 1/2 tablespoon of the butter. Combine remaining 2 tablespoons butter, crumbs, sugar and cinnamon in processor bowl with **steel blade**. Process until blended. Turn out into prepared pan. Press crumbs about one inch up sides. Leave a fairly thin layer covering bottom, and press lightly. Wipe out processor bowl with paper towel, and make filling.

FILLING

2 pkg. (8 ozs. ea.) cream cheese
2 thin strips lemon zest (3 x 1/2 in.)
1/3 cup sugar

3 eggs
3/4 tsp. almond extract
2 tbs. lemon juice

Cut cheese into chunks. Using **steel blade,** process strips of lemon with sugar. Add cheese and process until smooth. Scrape sides as necessary. Combine eggs, almond extract and lemon juice in measuring cup. Pour through feed tube with processor running. Stop and scrape sides. Process to smooth filling. Pour into crumb-lined pan. Bake in 350°F oven 35 minutes.

TOPPING

1 cup (1/2 pt.) sour cream
1-1/2 tbs. sugar

1/2 tsp. vanilla

Combine ingredients. Spread over baked cheese cake. Bake 10 minutes longer, or until topping is set. Cool, then chill. Makes 6 to 8 servings.

Chopping Meat

Being able to chop your own meat is one of the greatest pleasures a food processor has to offer. You know exactly the freshness and quality of the meat, and can control the amount of fat it contains.

I buy chuck roasts for chopped beef, pork loin or boneless shoulder roasts for chopped pork, and boneless legs of veal from New Zealand for chopped veal. They have good flavor and are often "on special." Trim away the heavy outside fat and tough connective tissue, leaving the inside fat. Since chopped meat needs fat for tenderness, juiciness and good flavor, replace the outside fat with about 2 tablespoons margarine, olive or vegetable oil, for each cup of meat cubes. You will have to experiment to find just the porportion of fat to meat that suits you best. (If you wish to avoid animal fat, trim away every bit of fat and replace it with whatever polyunsaturated oil or margarine you perfer.)

For even chopping, cut meat into 1-inch or smaller cubes or chunks. Chop, using the **steel blade.** Process with several "on-off" turns so you can watch the meat closely as it chops. Avoid chopping it too fine. For gauging amounts, one cup of cubes or chopped meat is 1/2 pound.

Steak Tartare

As you chop the meat for this recipe you'll realize how really fantastic a food processor is, and never want to buy ground meat again.

1/2 lb. lean top round or sirloin steak
1/2 tsp. salt
1/8 tsp. freshly ground pepper
1 egg white
black bread, French rolls or bread

garnishes: 1/2 small onion, chopped
1 tbs. drained capers
2 tbs. chopped gherkins
lemon wedges or slices

Trim steak and cut in 1-inch chunks. Fit **steel blade** in processor bowl. Add meat chucks, salt and pepper. Place cover on bowl. Process with several "on-off" turns, watching meat closely as it chops. Don't make it too fine. Add egg white through the feed tube. Process only a second to blend. Mound chopped steak on two individual plates. Surround with garnishes. (If preferred, blend garnishes into the ground steak, and add Dijon mustard or catsup.) Serve with black or French bread. Makes 2 servings.

For Canapes—Cut rounds of bread. Generously mound with steak tartar. Decorate with garnishes.

Meat Loaf with Sweet and Sour Sauce

Especially good made with your own country sausage (page 30). Goes well with steamed rice.

1-1/2 cups fine dry bread crumbs
1 cup milk
1 clove garlic
2 sprigs parsley with stems
1/2 medium onion, cut in chunks
1/2 green pepper, cut in chunks
1-1/2 lbs. (about 3 cups) beef chuck cubes

1/2 lb. coutry-style sausage
1 egg
1-1/2 tsp. salt
1-1/2 tbs. Worcestershire sauce
1/4 tsp. Tabasco sauce
2 to 4 tbs. oil

Combine crumbs and milk. Using **steel blade,** chop garlic, parsley, onion and green pepper finely. Add to crumb mixture. Without washing bowl, process meat in two or three batches. To the last batch of beef, add sausage, egg, salt, Worcestershire sauce and Tabasco. Process briefly to blend. Add to crumb mixture, along with rest of beef. Blend well with hands. Shape into two loaves. Place in shallow baking pan. Bake in

350°F oven 45 to 50 minutes. Serve on platter with Sweet and Sour Sauce spooned over and around loaves.

SWEET AND SOUR SAUCE

1 or 2 cans (20 ozs. ea.) pineapple chunks
1-1/2 green peppers
1/2 cup brown sugar
4 tbs. cornstarch
1/3 cup cider vinegar
2 tbs. soy sauce

Drain pineapple. Add water, if necessary, to juice to make 2 cups. Set aside. Cut green peppers into 1-inch squares or strips. Combine brown sugar, cornstarch, vinegar, soy sauce and reserved juice. Whisk over medium heat until mixture comes to a boil. Continue stirring, and boil 3 minutes. Add pineapple and green pepper. Reheat to boiling. Serve with meat loaf and rice. Makes 8 servings.

Country Sausage

Making sausage is easy with a food processor. What a pleasure to season it just the way you like. And you'll have juicy sausage to serve without a panful of fat to throw out! This is my favorite recipe.

2-1/2 lbs. lean country ribs or pork loin end roast
2 tsp. salt
1 tsp. ground pepper
1 tsp. grated fresh ginger root
or 1/2 tsp. ground ginger
1 tsp. crumbled dried sage leaves
or 1/2 tsp. powdered sage or poultry seasoning
1/2 tsp. sugar
1/4 tsp. ground cloves

Cut pork, including fat, into 1/2 by 1-inch pieces. There should be about 4 cups. Combine salt, pepper, ginger, sage, sugar and cloves. Sprinkle over pork pieces and stir to blend. (Mixture can be refrigerated for one to two days, if desired.) When ready to make sausage, insert **steel blade** in processor bowl. Add about 1 cup pork pieces and process 30 to 40 seconds. (Meat hitting the blades makes a smooth sound when it is uniformly chopped. If you should notice a loud sound, stop processor. Check blades for small pieces of bone or cartilage.) Transfer ground pork to a mixing bowl. Repeat until all pork is chopped. Shape into 8 large patties or 16 to 20 small ones. Brown over medium-high heat. Reduce heat to medium or low as patties cook on second side. Small patties take 10 to 15 minutes to cook, and the large ones about 20 minutes. Makes 8 servings.

NOTE: Set pork bones aside for some other use, such as barbecued bones, to cook with sauerkraut, or for beans with pork, etc.

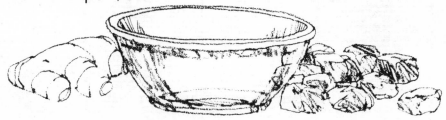

Blending • Slicing • Shredding
Chopping • Puréing

The recipes in this section were selected to futher acquaint you with the versatility of the food processor steel blade and discs. They are arranged according to the procedure used in their preparation.

Blending (steel blade) page 34—Shorter processing time than for chopping. Used when lighter mixing is desired as for egg salad, mayonnaise and other light mixtures.

Slicing (slicing disc) page 42—You'll have fun with this one. It quickly makes beautiful, even slices. It is helpful to buy vegetables that will fit into the feed tube without needing to be trimmed.

Shredding (shredding disc) page 54—Absolutely fantastic for soft cheese or vegetables, such as zucchini for zucchini bread or carrots for carrot-raisin salad. Remember, buy the ones that fit into the feed tube!

Chopping (steel blade) page 65—This is the procedure most often used. Chopping your own meat is the greatest . . . chopping cranberries the most fun!

Puréing (steel blade) page 77—A continuation of chopping. When you want something really smooth, such as for pate or baby food, nothing does the job as quickly or as well. Small amounts are handled as efficiently as large.

 **⟨Blending⟩**

Mayonnaise

1 egg
1 tbs. vinegar or lemon juice
1/2 tsp. salt
1/4 tsp. white pepper
1 tsp. Dijon-type mustard
1 cup salad oil

Insert **steel blade** in food processor bowl. Add egg, vinegar, salt, pepper, mustard and 1/4 cup of oil. With processor running, add the remaining oil through feed tube. Add oil slowly at first, then in a steady stream. When all the oil has been added stop processor. If mayonnaise is too thick add a little hot water or lemon juice. If it is not thick enough let processor run a little longer. Store in covered container in the refrigerator. Makes 1-1/4 cups.

NOTE: Two egg yolks used instead of 1 whole egg will make a very thick mayonnaise. It may be thinned with 1 to 2 tablespoons hot water, if desired.

Mustard Mayonnaise

Especially good on hamburgers!

1 tbs. Dijon-type mustard
1 tbs. red wine vinegar
1/2 tsp. salt
1 egg
1 cup salad oil

Insert **steel blade** in processor bowl. Add mustard, vinegar, salt, egg and 1/4 cup oil. With processor running, add remaining 3/4 cup oil through feed tube. Add oil slowly at first, then in a steady stream. When all the oil has been added, turn off processor. If mayonnaise is too thick add a little hot water. If too thin, process a little longer.

Roquefort Cheese Ring

Excellent with aperitif wine or cocktails. Serve with small crackers or slices of French rolls or baguettes.

1 pkg. (8 ozs.) cream cheese
3 to 4 ozs. Roquefort cheese
1 envelope (1 tbs.) unflavored gelatin
1/4 cup cold water
1/8 tsp. salt
freshly ground white pepper
1 tsp. cognac
5 or 6 pimiento-stuffed green olives
2 tbs. snipped chives
1/2 cup whipping cream, whipped
watercress or butter lettuce

Remove cheeses from refrigerator at least an hour before using so they will be at room temperature. Sprinkle gelatin over cold water in a 1-cup measure. Set in hot water until gelatin is dissolved. Oil a 7-inch ring mold (or other small mold) of 2-cup capacity. Insert **steel blade** in processor bowl. Add softened cheese, salt, pepper and cognac. Process until creamy. Use several "on-off" turns and scrape sides as necessary. Cut a center slice from each of the olives and reserve for decorating the ring after un-molding. Drop the rest in with cheese mixture. Pour in gelatin. Process to chop olives and blend in gelatin. Snip chives with scissors or sharp knife to avoid bruising and, thus, changing their flavor. Add to cheese mixture. Give a quick "on-off" to blend. Whip cream in chilled bowl. Add about 1/3 to cheese mixture. Give another "on-off" then quickly fold cheese mixture into remaining whipped cream before mixture sets up. Spoon into mold. Tap to settle. Cover with plastic wrap. Chill at least 3 hours. Unmold by warming 7 seconds in hot water. Turn out onto lettuce-lined dish. Add springs of watercress. Serves 10 to 12 as an hor d'oeuvre or 6 as a first course or in place of salad.

Swiss Delights

Excellent to serve at a wine tasting party. Add a pâté, made as much as a week ahead, and a basket of colorful raw vegetables for make-your-own salads, with a dish of homemade mayonnaise for dressing. For dessert, offer fresh fruits along with a round of Brie or Camembert and a wedge of Roquefort.

1/2 cup water
3 tbs. butter
1/4 tsp. salt
1/2 cup flour
2 eggs
2 ozs. Swiss cheese
vegetable oil for frying

Cut butter in several pieces. Combine with water and salt in small saucepan. Heat to simmering over medium heat. Remove from heat. Add flour all at once. Stir vigorously with wooden spoon. Return to heat for 15 to 20 seconds. Insert **steel blade** in food processor bowl. Add cooked mixture. Give one quick "on-off." Add eggs.

Process until a smooth, satiny mixture forms. Add cheese and give another quick "on-off." Heat oil in saucepan or electric skillet to 350°. Ease rounded teaspoonfuls of cheese flavored pâte à choux into fat. Cook 5 to 8 minutes until nicely puffed and browned. For even browning, encourage them to roll over using a slotted spoon. Lift from fat. Drain on paper towels. Keep warm in 150°F oven as long as 1-1/2 hours.

Whipped Cream Cheese

Spread generously on squash, pumpkin or cranberry bread. Try it on crackers or toast, topped with fresh strawberry jam! Use on sandwiches instead of mayonnaise . . . an especially good idea if you plan to freeze them.

1 pkg. (3-ozs.) cream cheese
1 to 1-1/2 tbs. heavy cream
few gratings fresh nutmeg

Cut cream cheese into several pieces. Using **steel blade,** process cheese a few seconds. Scrape sides of bowl. Process again, adding cream slowly through feed tube. Stop and scrape sides. Add nutmeg. Process a few seconds longer. Use immediately, or cover and refrigerate up to one week.

Variations:
Substitute 1/8 teaspoon dried dill weed for nutmeg. Nice on crackers or with fish.
Substitute 1-1/2 to 2 tablespoons undrained crushed pineapple for cream.

❮ Slicing ❯

Cucumbers Vinaigrette

2 or 3 sprigs parsley
1 clove garlic
1/4 tsp. salt
few grinds pepper
1 tbs. wine vinegar

3 tbs. olive or salad oil
1 large or 2 small cucumbers
1/8 tsp. dry dill weed
1 tsp. snipped chives, tarragon,
  basil or any fresh herb, optional

Wash parsley, and dry by squeezing it in paper towel. Make two or three cuts through parsley with sharp knife. Cut garlic in two or three pieces. Using **steel blade** process parsley and garlic until finely chopped. Add salt, pepper, dill, wine vinegar and olive oil. Process with an "on-off." Remove **steel blade,** and replace it with **slicing disc.** Leave dressing in processor bowl. Peel cucumbers. If too large to fit in feed tube, split in half lengthwise, and remove seeds with a teaspoon. Cut crosswise, stand vertically in feed tube, closely, but not tightly. Use pusher while slicing. Remove slicing disc. Stir cucumbers to mix with dressing. Turn into serving dish. Sprinkle with fresh herbs.

Fresh Pickle Slices

These refrigerator pickles are made with uncooked brine. It takes a few days for the full flavor to develop, but they taste awfully good almost immediately! With a food processor for speedy slicing, it couldn't be easier!

5 medium slender cucumbers
2 medium onions, peeled
2 cups sugar
2 cups cider vinegar

1/4 cup salt
1 tsp. curry powder
1/2 tsp. celery seed
1 tsp. mustard seed

Scrub cucumbers but do not peel. Fit **slicing disc** into processor bowl. If cucumbers are too fat to fit feed tube, remove a lengthwise slice with a vegetable peeler or knife. Slice cucumbers. Cut onions in halves and slice. Toss onions and cucumbers together to mix well. Put into two 1-quart or four 1-pint jars. Combine sugar, vinegar, salt, curry powder, celery salt and mustard seed. Stir to dissolve. Do not heat. Drain as much liquid from as possible from cucumbers. Pour pickling mixture in jars to cover cucumbers. Cover and refrigerate. Makes 2 quarts.

Marinated Mushrooms

For a unique salad, serve on leaves of butter lettuce. Tightly closed mushrooms are the freshest and will slice nicely with a food processor. Tired, limp mushrooms should be sliced by hand (or left at the store).

1-1/2 lbs. mushrooms
1 small onion
1 large clove garlic
2 tsp. (10 to 15 leaves) chopped fresh basil
or 1/2 tsp. dried sweet basil

1/3 cup lightly packed parsley
1/2 tsp. salt
1/4 tsp. freshly ground pepper
2 tbs. wine vinegar
4 tbs. olive oil

Wash and dry mushrooms. With **slicing disc** inserted, slice mushrooms, and transfer to large bowl. Change to **steel blade.** Cut onion and garlic into chunks, and add to processor bowl along with parsley, basil, salt and pepper. Process to a puree. Add vinegar and olive oil, and blend. Pour over sliced mushrooms. Stir gently and refrigerate. Use within about 3 hours. When ready to serve lift mushrooms from marinade with a slotted spoon, and allow to drain slightly. Place on lettuce if serving as a salad. Makes 6 to 8 servings.

Mushrooms Au Gratin

Serve hot as a meat accompaniment or as a luncheon dish.

2 slices day-old white bread (not dry)
1/4 lb. (1 cube) butter

Marinated Mushrooms, page 44
3 tbs. grated Parmesan cheese

Tear bread into pieces. Process with **steel blade** to make 1 cup soft bread crumbs. Add 2 tablespoons butter, preferably softened. Process until butter and crumbs are mixed. Coat a shallow baking dish heavily, using 2 tablespoons butter. (Individual au gratin or souffle dishes may be used, if desired.) Drain mushrooms, and discard marinade. Heat large skillet, and add remaining 4 tablespoons butter. When foam subsides, add drained mushrooms, and cook on highest heat 1 to 2 minutes. Stir. Reduce heat to medium-low. Cover, and simmer 10 minutes. Spoon mushrooms into baking dish. Pour any remaining liquid over mushrooms. Sprinkle with buttered bread crumbs and Parmesan cheese. Bake 10 to 15 minutes in the upper level of a 400°F oven. If crumbs aren't browned when mushrooms are hot, set under heated broiler a few minutes. Watch carefully. Makes 6 servings.

Carrots with Herbs and Madeira

Fresh herbs provide wonderful taste treats and can make the difference between excellent and mediocre cooking.

1-1/2 lbs. slender carrots
3 tbs. butter
3/4 tsp. <u>each</u> salt and sugar
2 tbs. Madeira wine
fresh chives, tarragon, parsley

Peel carrots, or scrub well Cut into 3-inch lengths. Insert **slicing disc** into processor bowl. Arrange cut carrots snugly in feed tube in vertical position. Use pusher with moderate pressure to slice carrots. Melt butter in heavy saucepan. Add carrots, salt, sugar and Madeira. Cover and cook over medium heat until steam begins to escape. Lower heat. Cook 10 minutes. Shake pan occasionally, holding lid in place. Transfer to warm serving dish, and sprinkle with about one teaspoon chopped fresh chives, tarragon, and/or parsley. If fresh tarragon isn't available, combine 1/8 teaspoon crumbled dried tarragon with fresh parsley and chives. Makes 6 servings.

Scalloped Potatoes

After you've had fun learning to slice potatoes, try this recipe.

6 tbs. butter	1/8 tsp. <u>each</u> nutmeg and white pepper
2 cups milk	6 medium russet potatoes
1 tsp. salt	3 tbs. flour

Use one tablespoon butter for coating the inside of a shallow 2-quart (7-1/2 x 12-inch) casserole. Heat remaining butter, milk and seasoning slowly in saucepan over low heat. Peel potatoes. Trim them, if necessary, to fit into feed tube. (Long, slender russets of medium size usually fit without trimming.) Slice potatoes, using **slicing disc.** Arrange half of potato slices in buttered casserole. Sprinkle half of flour over them. Scatter remaining potatoes over top. Sprinkle with rest of flour. Carefully add very hot or boiling milk mixture. Milk should be even with the top potato slices. Cover with casserole lid to waxed paper, and then foil. Bake in 350°F oven for 1 hour and 15 minutes. Uncover, and place under broiler to brown top. Makes 6 servings.

Apple Crisp

1/2 cup flour
1/2 cup brown sugar
1/2 cup oatmeal
6 tbs. (3/4 cube) butter, cut in slices
1/4 tsp. baking powder
1/8 tsp. salt

1/4 cup walnuts, optional
6 medium cooking apples
3 to 6 tbs. sugar
1/2 tsp. cinnamon
2 tbs. lemon juice
sweetened whipped cream

With **steel blade** inserted, add flour, brown sugar, oatmeal, butter, baking powder and salt to processor bowl. Process until mixture no longer looks "floury." Add walnuts and process just a second. Empty mixture into a bowl. Halve and core apples. Peeling not necessary. Without washing, reassemble bowl with **slicing disc**. Slice apples. (If any large pieces of apple skin should become lodged on **slicing disc**, remove and discard.) Arrange apple slices in buttered shallow baking dish. Combine sugar (adjusted to tartness of apples) and cinnamon. Spread over apples. Sprinkle with lemon juice. Distribute topping over all. Press down lightly. Bake at 350°F for 45 minutes. Serve warm, topped with whipped cream. Makes 6 servings.

Swiss Steak a La Robert

1 3-lb. round steak	1 cup red or white wine
2 medium onions	1-1/2 tsp. salt
1 stalk celery	1/2 tsp. pepper
1/4 lb. mushrooms	3 tbs. flour
3 tbs. <u>each</u> oil and butter	1 to 1-1/2 cups sour cream

Cut steak in serving-size pieces. Cut onions in half and celery in thirds to fit feed tube. With **slicing disc** inserted, slice onions, celery and mushrooms. Heat 1 tablespoon each oil and butter in a medium-size skillet over medium heat. Cook vegetables until translucent, about 5 minutes. Add wine, salt and pepper. Simmer while meat browns. Heat remaining oil and butter in large skillet over high heat. Brown pieces of steak. Remove from pan. Add flour to fat remaining in pan. Cook 1 to 2 minutes. Add hot wine-vegetable mixture. Stir to loosen brown particles from bottom of skillet. Blend in sour cream. Return pieces of steak and any juices which have accumulated to skillet. Cover, and simmer over low heat 45 minutes, or until very tender. Makes 6 servings.

		1	2	3
4	5	6	7	8	9	10
11	12	13	14	15	16	17
18	19	20	21	22	23	24
25	26	27	28	29	30	31

Baked Albacore with Hollandaise Sauce

Choose any firm fish of your liking. Bake an extra large piece so there will be enough left to make Fish Patties with Dill Sauce (page 160).

1 large piece (4 in. thick) albacore	freshly ground white pepper
1 <u>each</u> lemon and medium onion	3 tbs. butter
salt	Hollandaise Sauce, page 52

Insert **slicing disc** in food processor bowl. Slice lemon. Remove lemon slices and slice onion. Arrange onion slices in a small roasting pan with a cover. Lay fish on onion slices. Sprinkle generously with salt and freshly ground pepper. Dot with butter. Scatter lemon slices over top. Cover and bake in 375°F oven 45 minutes. Prepare Hollandaise sauce while fish bakes.

NOTE: Before storing leftover fish, remove bones. They come out more easily before chilling. Deglaze the roasting pan with a tablespoon or two of water or wine. Strain this flavorful juice over boned fish. Cover and refrigerate immediately for another delicious meal.

Hollandaise Sauce

Fabulous as it is, my food processor can't make Hollandaise. This recipe is a treasure and was taught to me by Chef Narces at Cordon Bleu, Paris. It makes the lightest, fluffiest Hollandaise sauce I have ever eaten. I have never had a failure or been disappointed with the texture or flavor. What more can I say? I hope you find the same success. This recipe can be increased by one-half or doubled successfully.

1/2 cup (1 cube) butter
2 egg yolks
2 tbs. water
1/8 tsp. salt
freshly ground white pepper
freshly grated nutmeg
few grains cayenne
1 to 2 tsp. lemon juice

Melt butter over medium heat. Set aside. Combine egg yolks and water in a small heavy saucepan. Place over medium heat. Whisk, with a small whisk that "fits" into the curve of the pan, until a very fluffy, slightly thickened mixture is formed. (This fluffy mixture is called sabayon.) Be alert and ready to lift pan from heat, whisking all the time. Keep in mind that the egg yolks must cook to thicken, but will curdle if they reach boiling. Whisk sabayon 10 to 20 seconds after removing from heat to make certain heat retained in pan doesn't curdle mixture. Cover sabayon and set aside to cool a bit. Butter and sabayon should be at about the same temperature when combined. You should be able to touch the sides of each pan without burning your hands. Set sabayon pan on a damp dish cloth to keep it from moving around. Whisk briskly while slowly adding the melted butter. Do not add the milky liquid in the bottom of the pan. Whisk in salt to taste (it usually needs very little), pepper, nutmeg and cayenne. Add lemon juice to taste. Cover and keep in a slightly warm spot if not using immediately. I have kept it nicely on the back corner of my range for as long as two hours.* Makes about 3/4 cup.

*A point to remember is that butter sauces, such as Hollandaise and Bearnaise (page 171) should be served warm, not hot. They can sit at room temperature for a while or can be held in a hot tap water bath . . . never over boiling or even simmering water.

❬ Shredding ❭

Cheese Fondue

In Switzerland pieces of Gruyere and Emmenthal cheese for a fondue are often bought in several different shops in an attempt to achieve the best blend of flavors and texture. For a wonderful light, wintertime meal or evening snack, serve cheese fondue with white wine, cider or beer, one-inch cubes of French bread, cut so each has some crust on it, pickles, apples and pears. If more hearty fare is desired, add cubes of ham or rolled slices of ham or salami to be eaten with fingers.

1-3/4 lb. assorted Swiss cheeses
6 tsp. cornstarch
1 clove garlic
2 cups white wine
1 tbs. lemon juice
1/4 tsp. salt
freshly grated white pepper and nutmeg
2 tbs. Kirsch or cognac, optional

Shred or chop cheese using **shredding disc** and/or **steel blade** depending on the firmness of the different cheeses you are using (see page 15). You should have six cups when shredded or chopped. Toss cheese and cornstarch together in large mixing bowl. Cut unpeeled garlic clove in half. Rub the inside of a heavy saucepan (enameled cast iron, if possible) or ceramic fondue pot with cut edges of garlic. Discard garlic. Pour wine into pot. Add lemon juice unless you are using a very acidic wine. Heat over medium to medium-high heat until tiny bubbles appear on pan. When they start breaking away and rising to the surface, stir in handfuls of cheese. Add cheese slowly to avoid cooling the mixture too much. Keep temperature constant (medium to medium-high). When cheese is all melted add salt, pepper and nutmeg. Stir in Kirsch. Taste. A little more salt or a few extra drops of lemon juice may be needed. Keep warm over heating device for fondue pot or on warming tray. If fondue becomes too thick, a little more warm wine can be stirred in. Makes 4 main course servings or 6 to 8 snack servings.

Carrot Raisin Salad

An old favorite with streamlined preparation. A pleasant change from tossed green or fruit salad.

1 lb. carrots
1/4 cup raisins, rinsed
1/4 tsp. salt

3 to 4 tbs. mayonnaise*
leaf or butter lettuce

Peel carrots or brush briskly. Cut into 3-inch lengths. Insert **shredding disc** in processor bowl. Fit carrot pieces upright in feed tube. Shred carrots, using very little pressure on feed tube. Stop if excessive vibration should occur. Sometimes carrots tip and become wedged in feed tube. Stop and reassemble them upright, adding more carrots. Transfer shredded carrots to mixing bowl. Dry raisins on paper towels. Toss raisins and salt with carrots. Add mayonnaise to moisten. Toss with a fork to blend. Serve on lettuce-lined salad plates. Makes 6 servings.

*Mayonnaise made with fresh lemon juice and a 1/2 x 1-inch strip lemon zest is especially delicious for this salad.

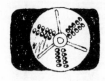

Creamy Potato Cheese Casserole

1 clove garlic
2 tbs. softened butter
2 ozs. Gruyère or Swiss cheese
1 egg
1/2 cup sour cream

1 cup milk
1-1/2 tsp. salt
1/8 tsp. <u>each</u> white pepper,
  nutmeg and dried thyme
7 medium potatoes, peeled

Cut unpeeled garlic in half. Rub interior of a 7-1/2 x12-inch rectangular casserole with cut edges of garlic. Butter generously. Shred cheese using **shredding disc.** Set aside. Whisk egg, sour cream, milk, salt, pepper, nutmeg and thyme together in small bowl. Still using **shredding disc,** shred potatoes. (If desired, potatoes may be sliced using the slicing disc.) Use firm pressure pusher to shred coarsely. Place half of potatoes in buttered dish. Sprinkle with half of cheese. Repeat with remaining potatoes and cheese. Pour egg-cream mixture over top. Shake dish gently to distribute liquid evenly through the potatoes. Bake in lower third of 375°F oven 50 to 60 minutes, or until potatoes are tender. If necessary, potatoes hold well in 150°F oven. Makes 6 servings.

 **Pizza**

If you have sauce made ahead and a partially baked crust ready, you can have pizza pretty fast.

Pizza Crust, page 140
Pizza Sauce, page 59, or purchased
3/4 to 1 lb. mozzarella cheese
toppings of your choice: salami, pepperoni, ham,
   ripe olives, green peppers, anchovies, etc.
2 tbs. grated Parmesan cheese
1/4 tsp. dried oregano or sweet basil
1 tbs. olive oil

Prepare crust and sauce early in the day. Shred cheese using **shredding disc.** Set 1/4 of the cheese aside. Spread sauce on pre-baked crust. Sprinkle with cheese. Add toppings. Cover with remaining cheese. Crumble oregano over cheese and dribble with olive oil. Bake in 400°F oven 15 to 30 minutes, until cheese is bubbly and crust nicely browned. Makes 6 generous servings.

Pizza Sauce

1 clove garlic, cut in half
1 medium onion, quartered
2 tbs. oil
2 cans (8 ozs. ea.) tomato sauce with tomato bits
2 tbs. catsup
1/2 tsp. <u>each</u> oregano and rosemary
salt and pepper to taste
2 tsp. Pesto, page 71, optional

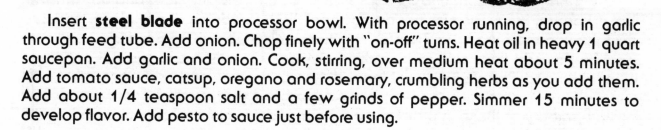

Insert **steel blade** into processor bowl. With processor running, drop in garlic through feed tube. Add onion. Chop finely with "on-off" turns. Heat oil in heavy 1 quart saucepan. Add garlic and onion. Cook, stirring, over medium heat about 5 minutes. Add tomato sauce, catsup, oregano and rosemary, crumbling herbs as you add them. Add about 1/4 teaspoon salt and a few grinds of pepper. Simmer 15 minutes to develop flavor. Add pesto to sauce just before using.

Zucchini Bread

1 tsp. shortening
2 medium zucchini (1-1/2 cups shredded)
2 cups flour
3/4 tsp. _each_ salt and baking soda
1/2 tsp. baking powder
1-1/2 tsp. cinnamon
_or_ 1 tsp. grated lemon zest _and_ 1/2 tsp. nutmeg

1 cup sugar
2 eggs
1/2 cup oil
1-1/2 tsp. vanilla
_or_ 2 tbs. sherry
1/2 cup walnuts

Use shortening to coat ends of 5 x 9-inch loaf pan well. Line sides and bottom with waxed paper. Scrub zucchini, but do not peel. With **shredding disc** in place, add zucchini through the feed tube. Transfer to a large mixing bowl. Reassemble bowl with **steel blade.** Add flour, salt, soda, baking powder, cinnamon and sugar. Cover feed tube with hand. Process just until blended. Remove cover, and add eggs, oil, vanilla and walnuts. Process only until blended. Add to bowl with zucchini. Stir to blend. Pour into prepared pan. Bake in 325°F oven 1 hour and 15 minutes, or until bread shrinks slightly from sides of pan. Makes 1 loaf.

Ollie's Carrot Cake

1 cup walnuts
4 medium carrots
1 cup crushed pineapple
2 cups sugar
3 eggs
1 cup oil

1/2 tsp. salt
2 tsp. vanilla
2 cups flour
2 tsp. each soda and cinnamon
1 cup coconut

Butter a 9 x 12-inch pan. Set aside. With **steel blade** inserted in processor bowl, chop nuts coarsely. Set aside. Switch to **shredding disc.** Cut carrots into 3-inch lengths. Stand snugly in feed tube. Use light pressure on pusher while shredding. Transfer shredded carrots to medium-size mixing bowl. Stir in pineapple, sugar, eggs, oil, salt and vanilla. Mix well with wooden spoon. In sifter combine flour, soda and cinnamon. Sift into carrot mixture. Stir. Add walnuts and coconut. Mix thoroughly. Turn batter into greased pan. Bake just below the middle of 375°F oven 45 minutes to 1 hour. Dust with powdered sugar. Serve with whipped cream or ice cream, as desired. Makes 12 to 18 servings.

Grandma Thomason's Steamed Pudding with Whiskey Sauce

When the food grinder replaced hand grating and chopping, it was considered a great "timesaver." What would our great grandmothers think of the speed and convenience of today's food processor?

3 tbs. soft butter
1/2 cup walnuts
1 cup pitted dates
<u>or</u> 3/4 cup raisins
2 medium carrots

1 large potato
2 eggs
1/4 tsp. salt
1 cup brown sugar
1 tsp. vanilla

1 tsp. soda mixed with
  2 tbs. hot water
1 cup flour
1 tsp. cinnamon
1/2 tsp. ground cloves

Butter a 6-cup mold with 1 tablespoon of the soft butter. Melt remaining butter and set aside. Using **steel blade** chop walnuts coarsely. Transfer to a medium-size mixing bowl. Cut dates in halves lengthwise. Add to nuts. Change to **shredding disc.** Shred carrots and potato using very light pressure on pusher so shreds will be fine. Add to mixing bowl with nuts and dates. Add eggs, salt, brown sugar, vanilla and soda dissolved in hot water. Mix all ingredients together well with wooden spoon. In sifter combine flour, cinnamon and cloves. Sift into mixing bowl with other ingredients. Stir to blend. Turn batter into buttered mold. Pour melted butter over top of pudding. Cover with lid or a double thickness of foil tied securely with string. Set on rack or jar rings in deep kettle with lid. Add boiling water to kettle until it reaches halfway up sides of mold. Cover kettle and steam 2-1/2 hours. Keep water boiling gently and replenish if needed. Serve warm. To unmold place a serving plate over top of mold. Reverse and give a quick shake if necessary to "encourage" it out of mold. Serve with Whiskey Sauce or Vanilla Butter Sauce, page 149. Makes 10 or more servings.

WHISKEY SAUCE—Combine 1/4 pound butter and 1 cup sugar in top of double boiler over boiling water until very hot. Add 1 beaten egg to hot mixture, whisking briskly until blended. Keep warm over simmering water. Add 2 tablespoons whiskey just before serving.

NOTE: Pudding can be refrigerated, still in mold, after steaming. Reheat in same kettle over simmering water for 1-1/2 hours.

❬ Chopping ❭

Fresh Cranberry Relish

Nice to share at holiday time. Makes a delightful "from-my-kitchen" gift.

2 small to medium red-skinned apples
1 large or 2 small oranges
3 cups firm fresh cranberries
1-1/2 cups sugar
1/8 tsp. salt
1/2 cup pecans, optional

Wash fruit. Quarter apples, and cut into chunks. Cut oranges, with rinds intact, into chunks. Remove seeds. With **steel blade** inserted in processor bowl, chop cranberries in two batches. Transfer to a large mixing bowl. Process apples and oranges, a few chunks at a time, until finely chopped, but not pureed. Empty each batch into bowl with cranberries. Add sugar and salt. Stir to blend. Place in covered container and refrigerate. Keep relish pressed below juices. A lovely red color develops as relish stands a few days. Will keep up to one month. At serving time sprinkle with chopped pecans, if desired.

Merren's Mushroom Pâté

One of my students gave me a gift of this spread, and then thoughtfully responded to my "thank you" with the recipe. Its simple preparation belies its elegance. Serve with melba toast, small crackers or cocktail rye bread.

1/2 lb. mushrooms
2 tbs. butter
1 medium onion, quartered
1-1/2 tbs. lemon juice
1 tsp. Worcestershire sauce
1/2 tsp. salt
1/8 tsp. pepper
2 tbs. mayonnaise (approx.)

Wash and dry mushrooms. Melt butter in medium-size skillet over medium heat. Fit **steel blade** into food processor bowl. Add onion and process until finely chopped but not puréed. Several "on-off" turns are useful here. It gives you more control over the consistency of the food you are chopping. Add onion to melted butter. Reassemble

steel blade in bowl without washing either. Chop mushrooms in two batches. Small mushrooms can be left whole. Medium or large ones should be broken. I usually break them between my thumb and fingers into pieces no larger than 1-inch on a side, as I drop them into the processor bowl. Cover bowl and process mushrooms until finely chopped. Use "on-off" technique to avoid puréing the mushrooms. Add mushrooms to onions as they are chopped. Stir and add lemon juice, Worcestershire sauce, salt and pepper. Cook, stirring, over medium heat about 15 minutes, or until mixture becomes a grey paste with juices evaporated. The mixture should not brown. Cool. Add mayonnaise to moisten, and additional pepper if needed. Store in small souffle dishes or crockery pot. Chill. Makes about 1 cup.

Make-Ahead Meatballs

Freeze in family-size portions, and you are never without an excellent meal in a minimum amount of time. Just reheat in Sweet and Sour Sauce (page 29), Tomato Herb Sauce (page 74), Hungarian Paprika Sauce (page 75), or Brown Sauce (page 72). All the better if the sauce has been made ahead, too.

several slices dry bread
1 cup milk
1 or 2 cloves garlic
1 medium onion
1-1/2 lbs. lean beef
1-1/2 lbs. lean veal
1 lb. lean pork

3-1/2 tsp. salt
1 tsp. dried thyme
1 bay leaf, crumbled
3 tbs. brandy (optional)
4 eggs
or 1 cup egg whites

Using **steel blade,** process bread to make 2 cups fine crumbs. Transfer to large mixing bowl. Stir in milk. Process garlic and onion until finely chopped. Add to crumb mixture. Trim meat of all bone and gristle. Without washing bowl, process meat in small batches until finely chopped. To last batch of meat add salt, pepper, thyme, bay leaf,

brandy and eggs. Combine meat with crumb mixture. Mix thoroughly with hands. Shape into 1 inch balls, and place on rimmed baking sheets. Broil 3 inches from source of heat for about 5 minutes. Remove from broiler. Place in 500°F oven for 5 minutes. Cool, and refrigerate or freeze. Reheat in sauce when ready to serve. Meatballs in Sweet and Sour Sauce make an excellent hot hors d'oeuvre. Have picks handy for spearing meatballs, pineapple and green peppers.

NOTE: If meat mixture is prepared several hours before it is to be cooked, onion and garlic should be sautéed in 2 tablespoons butter or oil and then added to crumbs.

Savory Fish Fillets

An inexpensive, quick and delicious way to prepare fish.

3 slices fresh or dry bread
1 clove garlic
1 onion, cut in chunks
5 tbs. butter
1/2 tsp. tarragon

1/4 tsp. thyme
2 lbs. fish fillets (red snapper,
  ling cod, ocean perch, sole)
1 tsp. salt
1/4 tsp. freshly ground pepper

Using **steel blade,** process bread to make 1 cup crumbs. Set aside. With steel blades in motion, drop in garlic. Add onion and chop finely. Melt 4 tablespoons butter in skillet over medium heat. Add garlic and onion. Saute 5 to 8 minutes, but do not brown. Stir in tarragon and thyme. Coat a large shallow baking pan with remaining butter. Pat fish dry with paper towels. Sprinkle with salt and pepper. Arrange in single layer in baking dish. (Fold thin sole fillets in half before placing in pan.) Distribute onion mixture over fish. Sprinkle with crumbs. Bake in the upper third of a 500°F oven 12 minutes. Makes 6 servings.

Pesto Sauce

1 oz. piece Parmesan cheese
1/4 cup walnuts or pine nuts, optional
2 to 3 cloves garlic
1/3 cup olive oil

1 cup fresh sweet basil leaves*
1/2 tsp. salt
freshly ground black pepper

Insert **steel blade** in processor bowl. With processor running, drop cheese through feed tube. Measure 1/4 cup cheese into a mixing bowl. Set aside. Add nuts to processor bowl. Process briefly to chop, not pulverize. Pour into bowl with cheese. Without washing processor bowl, reassemble with the same blade. With processor running add garlic. Remove cover. Add olive oil and basil leaves. Process until nearly smooth. Pour into bowl with cheese and nuts. Add salt and pepper. Stir to combine. Add extra oil if mix is not slightly runny. Spoon into a one-cup jar. Jiggle spoon in jar to release all trapped air bubbles. Pour a little olive oil over the top after cleaning the side of jar of any pesto. Repeat process each time you use some of the pesto. Store in refrigerator. Keeps as long as a year.

*or 1 cup firmly packed parsley leaves plus 1 tablespoon dried sweet basil

Brown Sauce

1 small onion
1 small carrot
3 to 4 tbs. butter or meat drippings
2-1/2 cups beef or chicken broth
1/4 cup flour

1 bouquet garni, page 5
1 clove garlic
1 shallot

1 tbs. tomato paste
1 beef bouillon cube
freshly ground pepper

Cut onion and carrot into 1-inch chunks. Process with **steel blade** until medium-fine texture. Melt butter in heavy, medium-size saucepan. Cook chopped onion and carrot over medium to medium-high heat for at least 20 minutes, stirring from time to time, until vegetables are richly browned. Heat broth while vegetables are browning. Add flour to vegetables, and cook a few minutes until flour is lightly browned and smells toasted. Remove from heat, and whisk in hot broth. Add bouquet garni. Without washing bowl process garlic and shallot until finely chopped. Add garlic, shallot, tomato paste, bouillon cube and pepper to sauce. Reduce heat. Simmer 2 hours, stirring occasionally. If sauce becomes too thick, add more broth or water. If too thin, uncover and boil vigorously, stirring often, until desired consistency is attained. Lift bouquet garni out into a sieve, press juices out, and discard. Strain remaining sauce, but do not press on vegetables. Instead, gently twirl a whisk in the strainer to allow sauce to flow through the vegetables freely, without allowing any vegetable pulp to pass through. Add salt if needed. Refrigerate sauce, if not using immediately. Sauce keeps nicely for a week.

Variations:

Stroganoff Sauce—Add 1 cup sour cream and 1/4 pound sliced, sauteed mushrooms to Brown Sauce. Serve over meatballs or with leftover roast beef for a triumphant second appearance.

Sauce Bordelaise—Chop 2 or 3 shallots and boil with 1/2 cup Bordeaux wine (California Cabernet Sauvignon) until nearly all liquid is evaporated. Add to 1-1/2 cups brown sauce. Heat to boiling. Swirl in 2 tablespoons softened butter. Serve with rare roast beef or tender steaks.

Tomato Herb Sauce

2 cloves garlic
1 large onion
2 tbs. each butter and oil
3 tbs. flour
1 can (16 ozs.) tomato purée
1 can (6 ozs.) tomato paste
1 cup chicken or beef broth
1 tsp. salt
freshly ground pepper
bouquet garni, page 5
2 tbs. chopped fresh oregano
   sweet basil, tarragon and sage combined*
1 tsp. pesto, page 71 (optional)
1/2 to 1 tsp. sugar

With **steel blade** inserted, chop garlic by dropping cut cloves into spinning blades through feed tube. Cut onion into chunks. Process until finely chopped. Heat butter and olive oil in heavy, medium-size saucepan. Add onion and garlic. Saute 5 to 10 minutes over medium heat. Do not let brown. Add flour. Cook about one minute, stirring constantly. Add purée, tomato paste and broth. Stir well. Add salt, pepper, bouquet garni and half the fresh herbs. Simmer slowly, covered, for 1-1/2 to 2 hours. Stir occasionally. Just before serving, remove bouquet garni, press out juices, and discard. Stir in remaining fresh herbs, pesto and a few grinds of pepper. Add sugar to bring out flavor, and more salt if needed.

Variations:

   Mushroom Sauce—Saute 1/4 pound sliced fresh mushrooms briefly in 2 teaspoons each butter and oil. Add to Tomato Herb Sauce.

   Hungarian Paprika Sauce—Add 2 to 3 teaspoons sweet Hungarian paprika to Tomato Herb Sauce, along with the salt and pepper. Just before serving, stir in 1 cup sour cream. Heat, but do not boil. Goes with meatballs, braised beef and chicken. Serve with noodles.

*Use 1/2 teaspoon each if substituting dry herbs.

❮ Puréing ❯

Chicken Liver Pâté

1/3 lb. thinly sliced bacon
1/2 medium onion, cut in chunks
1 small garlic clove
1/2-in. cube fresh ginger
1/3 cup cubed pork fat or bacon
1-1/2 tsp. salt

1/2 tsp. <u>each</u> white pepper and ground allspice
1 lb. chicken livers, rinsed
1 egg <u>plus</u> 1 egg white
3/4 cup cream or evaporated milk
2 tbs. cognac
1/4 cup flour

Line a 4 by 8-inch or 3 by 9-inch loaf pan with bacon. Set aside. Insert **steel blade** in processor bowl. Add onion, garlic, ginger, pork fat, salt, pepper and allspice. Process until very finely chopped. Add chicken livers. Turn "on-off" a few times. Add remaining ingredients. Process until blended. Turn into prepared pan. Cover with waxed paper and a double layer of foil. Press foil around lip of pan securely. Set into another larger pan. Pour boiling water into the outer pan. Bake in a 325°F oven 1-3/4 hours. Serve warm or cold with crackers or French bread and pickles. Keeps well for a week.

Cream of Celery Soup

6 cups chicken stock
3 tall stalks celery (2 cups chopped)
1 small onion (1/2 cup chopped)
1 or 2 shallots or scallions
4 tbs. (1/2 cube) butter
3 tbs. Cream of Wheat
1/2 tsp. chervil or tarragon
few grinds white pepper
Enrichment: 2 egg yolks, beaten
　　　　　　　1/2 cup cream
3 sprigs parsley (2 tsp. chopped)
few leaves fresh chervil or tarragon, if available

Heat stock in a 3-quart pot. Cut celery into chunks. Using **steel blade,** process about half at a time, until quite finely chopped. Chop onion and shallot in same manner. Melt butter in skillet. Add chopped vegetables and cook over medium heat 5 to 10 minutes. Do not allow to brown. Sprinkle Cream of Wheat over vegetables. Cook 1 to 2 minutes longer. Add to hot stock along with chervil. Boil 20 minutes. Using **steel blade,** purée mixture 2 cups at a time. (Soup may be refrigerated at this stage.) Just before serving, reheat soup to boiling. Combine egg yolks and cream. Whisk into boiling soup. Remove from heat. Don't allow soup to boil after adding enrichment. A few grinds of white pepper added now is pleasant. Serve very hot, garnished with fresh parsley, chervil and/or tarragon. Makes 6 servings.

Variation:

   Cream of Zucchini Soup—Substitute 4 medium zucchini for celery. Cut them into chunks. Add cooked vegetables and zucchini to hot broth. Boil 20 minutes. Purée and complete soup as directed. Taste and add salt if needed. Serve very hot. Is also delicious served cold garnished with a spoonful of sour cream and a dash of dill.

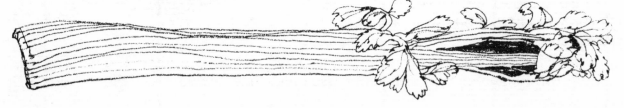

Cream of Tomato Soup

A special recipe from Cordon Bleu, Paris.

3 or 4 leeks
1/4 lb. butter
5 or 6 large fresh tomatoes
3/4 cup flour
8 cups boiling water
2 tsp. _each_ salt and sugar
1/4 tsp. freshly ground white pepper
2 to 3 tbs. tomato paste
Enrichment: 2 egg yolks, beaten
           1/2 cup whipping cream
1 to 2 tsp. snipped fresh chives
1/2 cup whipping cream, whipped
1/8 tsp. salt

Remove dark green tops from leeks. Use only white and very light green parts. Split tops in an "X," by inserting point of knife into white part of leek and running blade upward through top. Turn leek, and repeat at a 90° angle. (This allows layers to be separated and cleaned with running water.) Cut leeks into 3-inch pieces. With **slicing disc** inserted, stand leek pieces vertically in feed tube, and slice. (Loose top parts can be fitted in with firm bottom pieces.) Melt butter in large 3-quart pot. Add sliced leeks. Cook over medium heat, stirring occasionally, about 5 minutes, until translucent. Add tomatoes which have been peeled, seeded and chopped. Cook a few minutes. Stir in flour. Add boiling water. Stir with a whisk and then add salt, sugar, pepper and tomato purée. Cover, and cook 30 minutes at a slow boil, stirring from time to time. Using **steel blade,** purée 2 cups of mixture at a time. (Soup may be refrigerated at this point.) Just before serving, prepare enrichment by blending egg yolk with cream. Whisk quickly into very hot soup, and turn off heat. Soup should not boil after enrichment is added, as egg yolks will curdle. Taste for seasoning. Add salt if needed, and a grind or two of white pepper. Garnish with chives and lightly salted whipped cream. Makes 8 servings.

Pumpkin Soup

Make this the day after Halloween. What better way to say farewell to your jack-o-latern! Omit enrichment if you prefer a less creamy soup.

1 small pumpkin (4 cups cubed)
2 cups boiling water
1/2 tsp. salt
6 tbs. butter
1/2-in. cube ginger, peeled
or 1/4 tsp. ground ginger
1 medium onion, quartered
1-1/2 tsp. curry powder, optional
1/4 cup flour

4 cups chicken broth, heated
1-1/2 to 2 cups cooking liquid
freshly ground white pepper
freshly grated nutmeg
2 to 3 tbs. sherry, optional
Enrichment: 1/2 cup cream
2 egg yolks
1/2 cup whipping or sour cream
or croutons, for garnish

Cut pumpkin in half. Scrape out seeds and strings. Cut in strips to make peeling easier. Peel and cube. Combine pumpkin, water and salt in large saucepan. Cover and bring to a boil. Cook 15 minutes. With **steel blade** in place and processor turning, drop in ginger and onion through the feed tube. Chop finely. Use "on-off" turns to avoid puréing. Melt butter in 4-quart soup pot. Stir in ginger, onion and curry powder. Cook, stirring, over medium heat about 5 minutes. Blend in flour. Cook two minutes longer. Remove from heat. Whisk in heated chicken broth. Drain cooked pumpkin, saving cooking liquid. Purée pumpkin using same blade and bowl previously used. Add a little liquid if it seems necessary to make a smooth purée. Stir purée into soup. Add as much of the cooking liquid as is necessary to produce desired consistency. Season with pepper, nutmeg and salt if needed. Return soup to heat and bring to a simmer. Stir in sherry. To add enrichment, combine cream and egg yolks. Whisk into simmering soup. Heat but do not boil. Remove from heat and serve garnished as desired. If using whipping cream, whip it with 1/8 teaspoon salt. Makes 8 servings.

Variation—Fall colors in a soup bowl!

Omit ginger and curry powder. Add 1/2 sweet, red Bell pepper, chopped. Cook with onion and butter. Continue as directed.

Duchess Potatoes

A favorite when entertaining because they taste good, look pretty and can be prepared ahead. Also attractive as a decorative border on creamy seafood or chicken casseroles, or piped around planked steak or fish.

3 medium potatoes
2 tbs. butter
2 egg yolks
1/2 tsp. salt

freshly ground white pepper
freshly grated nutmeg
2 tbs. melted butter

Cut potatoes in halves. Cook in water to cover, without salt, for 20 minutes. Drain well. With **steel blade** inserted in food processor bowl, purée potatoes. Add butter, egg yolks, salt and nutmeg. Process only until smooth. Place potato mixture in a 16-inch pastry bag, fitted with large star tip (#4 Ateco). Pipe in decorative rings or ovals onto well-greased baking sheet. Refrigerate at this point, if desired. Just before serving, brush with melted butter. Heat in upper third of 400°F oven 10 to 12 minutes, until browned on ridges.

 **Almond Crusted Potato Patties**

Serve with poached or baked fish, or leg of lamb. Prepare ahead and reheat in the oven just before serving.

Dutchess Potatoes,page 84
2 tbs. soft or melted butter
1-1/2 cups sliced almonds

Prepare Dutchess Potatoes as directed. Butter a rimmed baking sheet. Spread almonds on waxed paper. Drop 6 rounded tablespoonfuls Dutchess Potato mixture, one or two at a time, onto almonds. Lift with fork or spatula to coat both sides of patties with almonds. Lay almond-coated patties on buttered pan. Patties can be refrigerated up to two days at this stage. Just before serving, bake in upper third of a 400°F oven, 10 to 12 minutes or until almonds on bottom are brown. Turn patties. Bake 5 minutes longer. Will hold in oven, with heat off, if necessary. Makes 6 servings. If desired, make 12 small patties allowing 2 per serving.

Carrot Purée

Carrots taste like a different vegetable.

2 lbs. carrots
2 cups water
4 tbs. (1/2 cube) butter
1 tsp. salt
freshly ground white pepper
freshly grated nutmeg
1 tsp. sugar

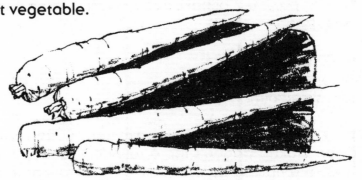

Cut carrots in 2 to 3-inch pieces. Place in saucepan with water. Cover and boil over medium heat 30 minutes. Drain. (Save water for soup or making bread.) Insert **steel blade** in processor bowl. Add carrots. Process about 2 minutes to make a smooth purée. Scrape sides of bowl. Add remaining ingredients. Process for one minute. Turn into souffle or other serving dish. Smooth top. Using knife or spatula make decorative ridges on top. Cover with foil and keep warm in 150°F oven or on warming tray. Holds well. Makes 6 servings.

Carol's Persimmon Pudding

1-1/2 tbs. soft butter
2 to 3 tbs. sugar
1 cup pitted dates
1 cup pecans or walnuts
3 to 4 ripe persimmons
2 cups sugar
2 tbs. melted butter

2 eggs
3 tsp. baking soda
2 tsp. cinnamon
1 tsp. <u>each</u> salt, allspice,
   nutmeg and cloves
2 cups flour
2/3 cup milk

Use soft butter to coat insides of two 4-cup molds or two 1-pound coffee cans. Dust with sugar. Empty out excess sugar. Cut dates in half lengthwise. Place in medium-size bowl. Coarsely chop nuts using **steel blade.** Mix with dates. Wash and dry persimmons. Pureé, using same blade and bowl. Add suagr, melted butter, eggs, soda, salt and spices. Process a few seconds. Add flour and milk. Process just long enough to blend. Combine with dates and nuts. Turn into prepared molds. Cover with lids or a double thickness of foil tied with string. Place on a rack or jar rings in a deep pot. Pour in boiling water to reach half way up sides of molds. Cover and steam 3 hours. Replenish water as necessary. Serve warm with Vanilla Butter Sauce (page 149) or whipped cream.

Cookies and Pastry

Cutting shortening into flour for shortbread-type cookies and pastry is accomplished with a food processor before you can get out your pastry blender. Anytime you encounter this procedure let your food processor do the job. In the beginning, you may feel most comfortable turning the flour-shortening mixture into a bowl and adding the liquid by hand. When you have mastered turning the processor off quickly, you will be ready to use it for blending in liquids. I guarantee you'll never go back to the "old fashioned" way. Just remember, to turn the processor off as soon as the dough feels and looks lumpy, which is almost immediately.

Crust for a pie or quiche can be ready for the oven in a fraction of the usual time. The same can be said for your favorite biscuits. Measure the dry ingredients and shortening into processor bowl. Process with **steel blade** until shortening is cut into flour. Pour liquid through feed tube and blend only until dough starts to gather into a ball. No further kneading will be necessary. Press or roll out. Cut using a biscuit cutter, or a large French knife for quicker "square" ones. Make horizontal and vertical cuts about 2 inches apart. You'll have square biscuits and no scraps to re-roll.

Shortbread Cookies

A perfect first venture into pastry making with food proessor.

1 lb. magarine or butter	1-1/4 cups sugar	5 cups flour

Because this is a large recipe it is easier made in two batches. It is baked in a rimmed 13 x 17-inch jellyroll pan or two 9 x 12 or 9 x 13-inch pans. Insert **steel blade** in processor bowl. Add 1/2 pound (2 sticks) margarine. Process until creamy. Scrape sides with plastic scraper. Add 1/2 cup sugar. Process to blend. Add 2 cups flour. Process with a quick "on-off." Add 1/2 cup flour. Process until blended. Mixture will be somewhat crumbly. Turn out on baking pan. Repeat with second batch using the same amounts and processing in the same way. Add to first mixture. Using hands, distribute evenly over baking sheet. Press with fingers. Smooth top with plastic scraper. Sprinkle with remaining 1/4 cup sugar. Prick with fork approximately every two inches. Bake in middle of 300°F oven 45 minutes, until a golden color. Remove from oven and immediately cut in diamonds. After cuttng, cookies can be left in pan to cool. Store in airtight container. Makes about 60 diamonds with small unevenly-sized pieces along edges for sampling!

French Butter Cookies

Just the thing to accompany fresh berries or sherbet. So quickly made, they are convenient to have in reserve for a sweet treat.

1 cup unsifted all-purpose flour
1/2 cup granulated sugar
1/2 cup (1 cube) butter, cut in 6 slices

1 egg yolk (large or extra large)
1 tsp. vanilla extract
or 1 tbs. rum or brandy

Place **steel blade** in processor bowl. Add flour, sugar and butter to bowl. Cover and process until butter is cut into flour and sugar, about 15 seconds. Put egg yolk and vanilla in a small dish. With processor running add through feed tube. Stop processor when dough gathers into a ball. This takes 15 to 20 seconds if butter was soft; one to two minutes if firm. Place ball on waxed paper. Form into a log two inches in diameter by 5 inches long. Roll paper around the log and chill until firm, about two hours. After chilling cut log in half lengthwise. Then slice into 1/8-inch half-circles. Place on ungreased baking sheet 3/4 inch apart. Bake in a 350°F oven about 8 minutes.

Crisp Butter-Nut Cookies

Before owning a food processor you might have hesitated to make anything with so many nuts to chop. Now the chore is done in seconds.

2 cups walnuts, pecans, almonds, filberts, or any combination of these
2 cubes (1/2 lb.) butter, softened
1/2 cup sugar
1/2 tsp. salt
2 tsp. vanilla extract
<u>or</u> 1 tsp. <u>each</u> vanilla and almond extract, if almonds are used in the cookies
2 cups flour
powdered sugar

With **steel blade** inserted, chop nuts finely, one cup at a time. Transfer to a large bowl. Add butter to processor bowl. (If butter is firm, cut each cube into 5 or 6 slices). Process until creamy. Add sugar, salt and flavoring to butter. Blend until light and fluffy. Scrape sides of bowl to insure thorough blending. Add flour. Process until dough forms a large lumpy ball. (If dough is reluctant to "go together," don't worry . . . just proceed as directed.) Turn dough into bowl with chopped nuts. Blend nuts in with wooden spoon, rubber scraper or your hands. To shape cookies, use about one tablespoon of dough for each cookie. Roll into a log the size of your little finger. Place on ungreased baking sheet and shape into a crescent. Bake in the upper level of 325°F oven 15 minutes, or until lightly browned. Remove to cooling racks. Sprinkle with powdered sugar. Cool, and store in tightly covered container. When ready to serve cookies, another light dusting of powdered sugar will enhance their attractiveness. Makes about 8 dozen.

Variations:

Coconut Logs—Substitute 2 cups grated unsweetened coconut for chopped nuts. Shape into logs 1/2 inch in diameter and 2 inches long. Bake in 400°F oven for 7 or 8 minutes. When cool, dust with powdered sugar, or dip ends of logs into 3 ounces semi-sweet chocolate melted with 1 tablespoon butter.

Easy-As-Pie Crust

This pastry is slightly easier to handle than the pastry for tartelettes (page 96). It is more tender but less flaky. Use for pies, tarts and quiches. It keeps well in the refrigerator for a week.

1 cube (1/4 lb.) firm butter
1 cube (1/4 lb.) firm margarine
2-1/2 cups all-purpose flour
1/2 tsp. salt
1 egg
2 tsp. lemon juice or white vinegar
3 to 4 tbs. cold water

Cut butter and margarine into 5 or 6 slices each. With **steel blade** in place, add flour, salt, and slices of butter and margarine to processor bowl. Process until butter is in small 1/4 inch pieces. Break egg into a measuring cup. Add lemon juice and enough water to make contents equal 1/2 cup. Beat with a fork to blend. With processor running, add liquid mixutre in a steady stream through the feed tube. Stop as soon as

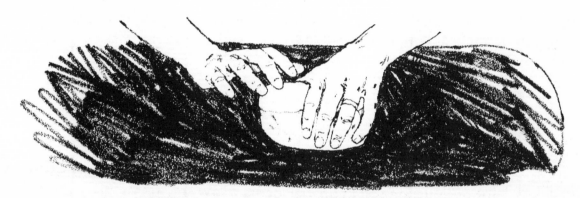

pastry gathers into a ball. Turn out onto waxed paper. Shape in two smooth, flattened balls leaving no cracks in edges. Wrap tightly in plastic or waxed paper. Chill 20 minutes or as long as one week. When ready to roll the well-chilled dough, let it sit at room temperature to soften slightly. Roll 1/8 inch thick. Fit into desired pans for pies, tartelettes or quiches. Chill again before baking to reduce shrinking. Bake at 400°F 12 to 18 minutes until lightly browned. Makes enough pastry for one 10-inch double crust pie, 30 3-inch tartelettes or two 10-inch quiche shells.

Pastry for Tartelettes

This is really fun to make! Keep a batch on hand . . . you'll use it for hors d'oeuvres, main dishes, desserts and many other things.

2 cubes (1/2 lb.) firm butter
2-1/2 cups all-purpose flour
1/2 tsp. salt
1/2 cup ice water (approximately)

Cut each cube of butter into 5 or 6 slices. Insert **steel blade** into processor bowl. Place slices of butter, flour and salt in bowl. Process a few seconds until butter is cut into small particles about the size of peas. (It is a good idea to use "on-off" turns often to check size of butter pieces.) With processor running, add water through feed tube. Stop adding when dough becomes lumpy. One to 2 tablespoons water will probably be unused. Let processor run a few seconds longer until dough gathers into a ball, then stop immediately. Remove dough and shape into two flattened rounds, using a little extra flour if necessary. Wrap in plastic. Chill 20 minutes in the freezer or about 1 hour in the refrigerator. When ready to roll and shape, pound dough with side of rolling pin if it is hard. Continue rolling to 1/8 inch thickness. Cut circles with a 4-inch round cutter or a 1-pound coffee can with both ends removed. Fit pastry circles into 3-inch tartelette pans. Prick bottoms with fork. Chill 20 minutes longer. (May be frozen at this stage.) Fit a smaller tartelette pan inside to help retain shape. Bake in 400°F oven 12 minutes. Remove lining pan and return to oven 5 more minutes. Makes 30 to 36 three-inch tartelettes.

NOTE: May be baked while still frozen. Follow the same timing.

Mushroom Tartelettes

Tartelette Shells, page 96
Duxelles, page 10
2-1/2 tbs. flour
1 cup heavy cream
1/4 tsp. grated nutmeg

salt and pepper
2 tsp. chopped fresh chives, tarragon,
    parsley or chervil or a mixture
paprika
grated cheese

Bake tartelette shells and set aside. Prepare duxelles as directed. Blend flour into duxelles. Add cream, nutmeg, salt and pepper. Cook, stirring, over medium heat until mixture boils and reaches a medium-thick consistency. Remove from heat. Stir in herbs. Spoon into baked shells. Sprinkle with a dash of paprika and a pinch of grated cheese. Serve warm. If necessary, reheat in a 350°F oven 5 to 7 minutes. If tartelettes are chilled, reheating should be increased by about 7 minutes. Makes 14 tartelettes of three inch diameter.

Lemon Tartelettes

For the ladies . . . small, beautiful and definitely worth the calories!

SWEET TART PASTRY

1-1/2 cups flour
1 cube (1/4 lb.) butter
1/4 cup powdered sugar
1/4 tsp. salt
3 egg yolks <u>or</u> 1 egg <u>plus</u> 1 egg yolk

Insert **steel blade** in food processor. Add flour, butter (cut in six slices, if it is not soft), powdered sugar and salt. Process a few seconds to blend. Add egg yolks and process with "on-off" turns until mixture forms a ball (or sticks together). Divide dough into 20 pieces of about one-inch diameter. Press into small fluted tart pans, 2-1/2 inches in diameter by 3/4 inch deep. Bake in 375°F oven 10 minutes, or until lightly browned. Gently turn tartelettes out onto rimmed baking sheet to cool.

continued

LEMON FILLING

6 tbs. sugar
zest of 1 lemon (remove with
 vegetable peeler)
1/2 cup lemon juice
1 egg
2 egg yolks
2 tbs. butter

   With **steel blade** in processor bowl, add sugar and lemon zest. Process until zest is finely chopped. Transfer to a heavy saucepan (enameled cast iron, if available) or the top of a double boiler. Add lemon juice, egg, egg yolks and butter. Whisk over medium-high heat (or simmering water if using double boiler) for 5 or 6 minutes, or until mixture thickens somewhat and "coats a spoon." It must not boil. Mixture will thicken as it cools. Distribute a small spoonful in each of the 20 tartelette shells. Top with meringue and finish as directed.

MERINGUE

3 egg whites (1/3 to 1/2 cup)
1/8 tsp. <u>each</u> salt and cream of tartar
1/2 cup powdered sugar
2 to 3 tbs. powdered sugar for tops

   Have egg whites at room temperature. Whip in copper bowl with a large whisk, or in small bowl with electric mixer. Add salt and whip, slowly at first, adding cream of tartar when whites are frothy. (Omit cream of tartar if using copper bowl.) When soft peaks form, whip in powdered sugar gradually. Continue beating until meringue forms stiff peaks. Transfer immediately to a large (16-inch) pastry bag fitted with a star tip of approximately 1/4-inch diamter (number 4 Ateco). Pipe meringue onto tartelettes in concentric circles, decreasing as you build a two-inch high peak of swirled meringue. Dust with powdered sugar. Brown in 325°F oven 6 minutes. Makes 20 tartelettes.

Walnut or Pecan Tartelettes

Pastry for Tartelettes, page 96
2 cups walnuts or pecans
1 cup sugar
1/8 tsp. salt
2 tbs. butter
3 eggs
1 cup dark corn syrup
1 tsp. vanilla
or 2 tbs. bourbon

Prepare pastry and roll about 1/8-inch thick. Cut with 4 or 4-1/2-inch round cutter. Drape into 3-inch tart or muffin pans. Do not prick pastry. Place in freezer while you prepare filling. It is important to chill pastry at this point to reduce shrinkage. With **steel blade** inserted, process walnuts or pecans with a few "on-off" turns. When coarsely chopped transfer to a bowl. Reassemble **steel blade** in processor bowl without washing either. Add sugar, salt and butter. Process to blend. Add eggs. With processor running add syrup and vanilla through feed tube. Add mixture to bowl with chopped nuts. Stir to blend. Spoon into chilled unbaked pastry. Bake in lower third of 400°F oven about 20 minutes, until pastry is lightly browned and filling slightly puffed. Let cool on racks a few minutes. Ease out of pans, using a small spatula or table knife. Continue cooling on racks. When cold, store in covered containers with waxed paper between layers. They will keep well for a week if well hidden! Makes 30 to 36 tartelettes.

Pâte à Choux

What to do with pâte à choux? Lots of things! Cream puffs can be made so quickly and effortlessly with the aid of a food processor they might be put under the heading of "old favorite revived." Make tiny puffs to freeze for a special occasion. They're easy to fill with a bit of chopped ham, chicken, turkey, crab or whatever, combined with mayonnaise (page 32). Prepare the filling while the puffs "freshen" and crisp in a 350°F oven for about 10 minutes. For an unusual dessert, combine whipped cream with a can of sweetened chestnut puree (marrons glace) and fill "freshened" puffs. Dust with powdered sugar or drizzle with caramelized sugar.

Don't stop there. Try some of the delicious recipes in this section, such as Potato Puffs (page 114), or Puffy Swiss Cheese Ring (page 110), in which pâte à choux is one of the ingredients.

Pâte à Choux

This is a "can't miss" recipe. Don't avoid cream puffs, or any delicious recipe which calls for pâte à choux, any longer! It's a cinch to make with a food processor. Where a smaller amount is needed, simply cut recipe in half.

1 cup water
1/4 lb. butter, cut in 5 or 6 slices
1/4 tsp. salt
1 cup all-purpose flour
4 eggs

Combine water, butter and salt in saucepan. Bring to boil over medium heat. Remove from heat and immediately add flour. Beat vigorously with a wooden spoon until mixture forms a ball. Return to heat for 15 to 20 seconds. Remove from heat. Place in processor bowl fitted with the **steel blade.** Add 2 eggs and process until blended. Add remaining 2 eggs and process until blended. Scrape sides of bowl and blend again briefly. Use for making cream puffs or in recipes calling for pâte à choux.

Cream Puffs

Pâte à Choux, page 106
1 egg white

Prepare pâte à choux as directed. Preheat oven to 425°F. Rub baking sheets light-ly with shortening. Spoon pâte à choux onto baking sheets in 12 evenly sized mounds leaving about 1-1/2 inches between each. <u>For small puffs</u>, make into 24 1-inch mounds. Lightly beat egg white. Brush onto each mound, shaping smooth half-spheres as you go. Bake in the upper third of oven 10 to 12 minutes until puffed, slightly browned, and crisp on sides. Reduce temperature to 375°F. Bake for an additional 10 minutes. For large puffs, reduce oven again to 325° for 10 minutes. For large puffs, reduce temperature again to 325°F for 10 minutes longer, or a total of about 30 minutes. For small puffs turn heat off and leave them in the oven 10 minutes longer. It is important to let puffs become very crispy on the outside so the slight moistness from inside does not soften the entire puff upon standing. Fill cooled puffs with whipped cream, ice cream or French Pastry Cream, page 109. Dust tops with powdered sugar. Makes 12 large puffs, 24 small puffs.

Small Cream Puffs
With Chocolate Sauce

24 small puffs, page 107
French Pastry Cream, page 109, or
   sweetened whipped cream
4 to 6 ozs. semi-sweet chocolate
4 to 6 tbs. water

Fill puffs by cutting off top third, or by inserting the tip (1/4 inch) of cream filled pastry bag into each puff and forcing in filling. Puffs may be filled and refrigerated 2 hours before serving. Combine chocolate and water in a heavy saucepan or double boiler. Heat until chocolate is melted. Whisk to blend. Sauce is best served warm and it may be reheated when needed. Makes 6 servings of 4 puffs each.

Sauce Variations:
   Use 4 to 6 tablespoons strong coffee instead of water.
   Use 2 to 3 tablespoons rum, brandy, mint or orange flavored liqueur and 2 to 3 tablespoons water instead of all water.

French Pastry Cream

Use extra large egg yolks for the smoothest, richest pastry cream.

1-1/2 cup milk
4 large or extra large egg yolks
1/2 cup sugar
1/8 tsp. salt
1/4 cup flour
2 tbs. butter
1 tsp. vanilla

Heat milk to boilng, Beat egg yolks, sugar and salt together in a heavy saucepan. Blend in flour. Slowly stir in boiling milk. Cook over medium to medium-high heat, stirring constantly, until mixture boils for about 2 minutes. Remove from heat. Stir in butter and vanilla. Prevent a skin from forming on the top by covering with plastic wrap pressed against surface of filling. Cool and fill puffs, or chill if desired. Whisk filling before using if it has been refrigerated.

Puffy Swiss Cheese Ring

As dinner guests of a French family in a Paris suburb near Chateau de Sceaux, my husband and I were served wedges of this cheese ring as a first course, followed by rare roast beef. A fine bordeaux wine accompanied both courses.

4 ozs. Swiss or Gruyère cheese
1 egg or 1 egg white for glazing
Pâte à Choux, page 106
freshly grated nutmeg

Adjust oven rack 1/3 distance from top of oven. Preheat oven to 425°F. Cut cheese in 1/2-inch cubes. Insert **steel blade** in food processor bowl. With blade in motion, add cheese through feed tube. Set cheese aside. Lightly grease and flour a large baking sheet. Using a pot lid or cake pan, mark an 8-inch ring in the flour coating. Fit a 16-inch pastry bag with a 1/2-inch round tip (a spoon can be used). Beat egg lightly with fork. Set aside. Prepare pâte à choux as directed using **steel blade.** Add cheese and nutmeg. Process just to blend. Fill pastry bag with mixture. Pipe three ridges using guide marked in flour. Two go side-by-side, the third is laid on top where the first two

touch. If using a spoon instead of a pastry bag, place large spoonfuls close together around marked ring. With a soft pastry brush, coat top with beaten egg, smooth out any ridges. Bake in 425°F oven 25 minutes. Reduce heat to 375°F and continue baking 10 to 15 minutes until crisp and nicely browned. Cut in modified wedges. Makes 8 to 12 servings.

Potato Gnocchi

A make-ahead potato dish. Different and tasty . . . a good choice for a dinner party.

2 ozs. Swiss or Gruyère cheese
1/2 recipe Pâte à Choux, page 106
3 medium potatoes
1/2 tsp. salt
freshly ground white pepper
freshly grated nutmeg
2 tbs. melted butter

Fit **steel blade** into processor bowl. Process cheese until finely chopped and you have 1/2 cup. Set aside. Prepare pâte à choux as directed, substituting milk for water. Set aside in a mixing bowl. No need to wash processor bowl or blade. Peel and halve potatoes. Boil in water to almost cover, without salt, for 20 minutes. Drain well. Place potatoes in processor bowl and purée using **steel blade.** Add salt, pepper, nutmeg and all but 2 tablespoons cheese. Add pâte à choux. Process just to blend. Turn out on-to floured flat surface. Use your hands to roll into 1-inch diameter tubes. Cut in 3-inch sections, like large corks. In large deep skillet, heat 2 quarts water with 4 teaspoons salt, to simmering. Add gnocchi using a slotted spoon. Adjust heat to keep water just at simmering. Hard boiling will break gnocchi, in which case you would end up with potato soup. After 10 minutes, when gnocchi are floating on the surface, remove with slotted spoon. Drain on folded soft towel. Assemble, single layer, in buttered, shallow oven-to-table dish. Dribble with melted butter and sprinkle with reserved 2 table-spoons cheese. (Can be refrigerated at this point.) Bake in 375°F oven 30 minutes. Longer if made ahead and refrigerated.

Variation:

    Omit cheese in gnocchi. Sprinkle top with 2 tablespoons grated Parmesan cheese or 2 to 3 tablespoons buttered dry bread crumbs.

Potato Puffs

Tater Tots par excellance! Dutchess potatoes combined with pâte à choux and deep fried. Make small puffs for a different, very tasty hor d'oeuvre.

1/2 recipe Pâte à Choux, page 106
1 recipe Duchess Potatoes, page 84
oil for deep frying

Prepare pâte à choux. This can be done well ahead. If it has been refrigerated, bring to room temperature. Prepare Duchess Potatoes as directed, using **steel blade.** Add pâte à choux and process until blended. Heat oil to 360° in deep fryer, saucepan or electric skillet. Carefully drop potato mixture by rounded teaspoonfuls into hot fat. Cook 5 to 8 minutes, until browned. Turn any puffs that don't turn themselves. Drain on paper towels. Can be held in 150°F oven up to 1-1/2 hours. Makes 6 to 8 servings.

NOTE: For hor d'oeuvres, make puffs smaller. Fry about 5 minutes. Drain, and serve on folded napkin or doilie.

Fritters

Pâte à Choux, page 106
vegetable oil for frying

Prepare pâte à choux as directed. Heat oil to 360° in deep saucepan or deep fat fryer. Ease tablespoonfuls of pâte à choux (a rubber scraper is helpful) into hot fat. Do not crowd as they will expand. Fry about 8 minutes. Turn to brown evenly. Serve warm, sprinkled with powdered sugar, or fill with whipped cream, French Pastry Cream (page 109) or jam. Sprinkle with powdered sugar.

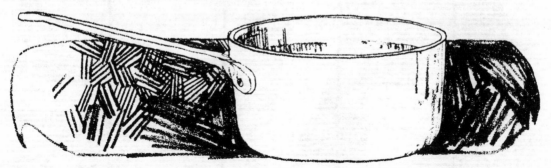

Puff Paste

If you've ever made puff paste in the traditional manner (or even read about how it is made) you know it is not an easy process. Little wonder it has achieved such a glamorous reputation. It is rarely made except for the most elegant or special occasions and is truly a labor of love.

Many find it difficult to believe there is such a thing as quick puff paste, but there is, with an assist from a food processor. If you've always wanted to "try your hand" at making puff paste, but hesitated, wait no longer. It can easily be made without having had past experience. You may not achieve perfection on the first attempt, but don't be too critical. It will be outstanding enough to make you proud of your accomplishments.

Puff paste is fun to work with and can be used in many exciting ways from Napoleons to Beff Wellington to disguising leftovers. Chicken or turkey, or flaked seafood in a cream sauce with mushrooms and a bit of sherry, served in a shell of buttery, flaky layers of pastry, becomes instantly special.

Puff Paste keeps in the refrigerator for several days or can be frozen.

Quick Puff Paste

Those who have made puff paste in the traditional manner are filled with awe and appreciation for this recipe. If you have always avoided puff paste, cast away your hesitations. You'll find pleasure when you "get into" the many special things you can create, now, with relative ease.

3 cubes (3/4 lb.) butter	1/2 tsp. salt
3 cups all-purpose flour	1-1/2 cups sour cream

Cut each cube of butter into 5 or 6 slices. With **steel blade** in place, add butter, flour and salt to processor bowl. Process briefly until butter is cut coarsely into flour. Remove cover and add sour cream. Process a few seconds until mixture forms a ball. Turn off instantly. Divide in half. Flatten and wrap in plastic. Refrigerate about an hour. When chilled, but not too firm, roll pastry into a rectangular shape approximately 6 by 16 inches and about 3/8 inch thick. Fold into thirds making a smaller rectangular shape. Rotate pastry 90°. Repeat the rolling and folding process. (You have just completed two "turns." You may make as many as 6 turns. Chill 30 to 40 minutes between each one or two "turns".) Wrap and chill until ready to shape. Can be kept up to 5 days in the refrigerator. Freeze for longer storage.

PUFF PASTE TIPS

It is usually rolled to slightly thicker than 1/8 inch.

Edges should always be trimmed if you want them to puff freely.

When baking, sprinkle baking sheet with cold water and turn pastries up-side down on sheet.

Most things glazed with egg are improved with 2 layers of glaze. Don't allow glaze to run down edges causing them to be glued together so they can't puff.

Always chill pastry after shaping and before baking.

Pastry goes directly from refrigerator or freezer to oven.

Pastry should always be put into upper third of hot oven to cause it to puff.

When puffed and browned, heat can be reduced by 50 degrees to finish drying it.

Pastry feels crisp on edges when it is done.

Puff paste, like home made bread, is best on the day it is baked.

It is always good, though perhaps not perfect at first. Don't be too critical.

 # Allumettes

Strips of pastry about an inch wide with a baked-on glaze of Royal Icing.

1 egg white
1 tsp. lemon juice
1-1/2 cup powdered sugar
Quick Puff Paste, page 118

To make Royal Icing, add lemon juice to egg white and stir in powdered sugar to make a spreadable icing. It is not fluffy. Keeps well in refrigerator for weeks. Roll pastry slightly thicker than 1/8-inch. Trim edges. Cut strips about 4 inches long and 1-1/4 to 1-1/2 inches wide. (Puff paste never spreads, in fact it shrinks as it puffs upward.) Turn strips over and brush off excess flour with soft pastry brush. Spread a thin layer of icing over entire surface. Place on cold water-sprinkled baking sheet. Chill in freezer 20 minutes or longer. Bake in upper third of 400°F oven 9 to 11 minutes. Watch carefully. Remove when icing looks like a perfectly toasted marshmallow. Cool on racks. Hide them if you want to see them again!

Sugar-Crusted Flaky Pastries

Simple when you have Puff Paste in your refrigerator.

Quick Puff Paste, page 118
granulated sugar

Let pastry sit at room temperature a while to soften slightly, or pound it with rolling pin to soften more quickly. Repeat pounding at 90° angle. This does soften it so it can be rolled without waiting. Roll no more than half of pastry at a time. Roll to 1/4-inch thickness. Cut with round, ripple-edged cutter of 2-1/2-inch diameter, or larger. Stack scraps in layers. Press together, chill and roll again. Clear an area on your rolling surface and pour about 1/2 cup granulated sugar. Lay cut circles top-side down in sugar. Roll over each circle with one firm motion stretching it to twice its length. Now it is an oval with sugar coating on one side. Reverse onto a cold water-sprinkled baking sheet. Chill or freeze 1/2 hour. Bake in upper third of oven 375°F for 10 to 12 minutes or until lightly browned.

Beef Filets in Flaky Pastry

Beef Wellington adapted for individual portions. Can be prepared as much as 24 hours ahead. Accompany with Broiled Tomatoes (page 23) or a simply prepared green vegetable such as fresh asparagus, or Brussels sprouts cooked ahead then tossed with lemon butter.

6 filet mignon steaks at least 1-1/4 to 1-1/2-inches thick
salt and pepper
1 tbs. <u>each</u> butter and oil
1/3 cup Chicken Liver Pâté, page 77
2/3 cup Duxelles, page 10
Quick Puff Paste, page 118
1 egg for glaze

Trim filets well of all fat and shiny outside skin which toughens when cooked. Salt and pepper filets. Heat butter and oil until very hot. Briefly cook filets, one minute or less per side. Chill. Spread pate, or place a slice of it, on each filet. Press duxelles into pâté. Roll pastry 1/8-inch thick. Cut in squares large enough to enclose a filet. Drape

squares diagonally over each filet and tuck ends under. It is not necessary to cover bottom completely. Pinch corners together. Beat egg until blended. Brush over pastry. If desired, cut pastry scraps in interesting shapes and decorate top of pastry. "Glue" to pastry with more egg glaze. Glaze decorations carefully so glaze does not run over edges. Cut a slit or hole in top of each pastry package to allow steam to escape. Refrigerate up to 24 hours. Glaze again just before baking. Bake in upper third of 425°F oven 20 minutes. Loosen with spatula and slide onto warm platter. Garnish with fresh watercress. Makes 6 servings.

Sherried Chicken Livers in Flaky Pastry

Sherried chicken livers, creamy Mornay sauce and buttery-crisp, flaky pastry, combine to make a fantastic luncheon dish, or a first course for an elaborate dinner, or the main course for a light but impressive dinner.

Quick Puff Paste, page 118
1 egg, beaten, for glaze
2-1/2 to 3 cups Mornay Sauce, page 9
2 lbs. chicken livers
2 shallots
2 tbs. <u>each</u> butter and oil
1-1/4 tsp. salt
freshly ground pepper
3 tbs. sherry or Madeira wine

Roll puff paste to slightly thicker than 1/8-inch (between 1/8 and 1/4-inch). Trim edges, then cut in 3 to 3-1/2-inch squares, rectangles or diamonds. (For diamonds, cut parallel to two of the edges. Cut diagonally the other direction.) Prick with point of knife. Glaze with beaten egg. Decorate by cutting designs in pastry with sharp knife or "glue" pastry scraps on top in a design. Chill 30 minutes. Glaze again before baking. Bake in upper third of 400°F oven 15 to 20 minutes. Prepare Mornay sauce. Heat in double boiler over simmering water for half an hour before serving. Rinse chicken livers with cold water. Drain. Cut each in 2 or 3 pieces. Dry on paper towels. Mince shallots using **steel blade.** Set aside. When preparing 2 pounds of chicken livers I find it easier to use two skillets to insure quick cooking. About 10 minutes before serving, heat skillets very hot with 1 tablespoon each oil and butter in each skillet. Add chicken livers in a single layer, not crowded. Cook about 6 minutes, adding salt, pepper and shallots during cooking. Add sherry. Ignite or boil for one minute. Shake pans to distribute flavor among livers. To serve, split warm pastries. Distribute sherried livers over bottoms. Spoon warm Mornay sauce over livers. Lay decorated pastry tops over sauce. Garnish each serving with a sprig of fresh tarragon, if available. Pass extra sauce in a warm sauceboat. Makes 6 to 8 servings.

Yeast Bread and Rolls

Lightening fast action by the food processor blades developes the gulten in flour giving yeast breads and rolls a nice texture, and saves you alot of kneading.

When making yeast breads use small recipes and avoid making dough too stiff for the food processor to handle easily. It may be necessary to knead some of the flour in by hand when a stiff dough is desired. However, kneading time is considerably reduced if the initial mixing is done with the food processor. No-knead recipes usually produce a softer dough and adapt extremely well to the food processor.

After trying some of the yeast breads and rolls in this section, adapt your own favorites to the food processor, applying the same techniques used in these recipes.

Rich Yeast Dough

This recipe makes tender, good-flavored yeast rolls. The dough can be used without chilling or can be refrigerated for a long as three days.

2 pkgs. active dry yeast
1/3 cup very warm (115°) water
1/2 cup (1 cube) butter or margarine
1 cup milk
4-1/4 to 4-3/4 cups all-purpose flour

1/3 cup sugar
2 tsp. salt
3 large eggs
2 tbs. melted butter

Add yeast to warm water in small bowl. Stir, and set aside. Cut butter into small pieces. Warm with milk in small saucepan over low heat. Warm unbroken eggs in a bowl of hot tap water. (Dough rises faster if all ingredients are warm.) With **steel blade** in place, measure 2-3/4 cups flour into processor bowl. Add sugar, salt, eggs, dissolved yeast, and warm milk/butter mixture. Butter need not be completely melted. Mix, by turning processor "on-off" a few times. Then let run about one minute. This develops the gluten, making traditional kneading unnecessary. Turn mixture out into a large mixing bowl. Stir remaining flour in by hand, using a wooden spoon. The amount of flour needed will vary with the brand using and the size of the eggs. The dough should be soft and sticky. Cover lightly with waxed paper or plastic. Let rise 1-1/2 to 2 hours at room temperature, or cover securely with plastic wrap. Refrigerate immediately. The dough will be easier to handle after chilling. To proceed without chilling, turn the dough (which has risen to double its original volume) onto generously floured surface. Pat lightly with floured hands (or use a very light touch on a floured rolling pin) to a thickness of one-half inch. Cut rolls with a 2-1/2-inch round cutter. Place on large 13 x 17-inch ungreased baking sheet. For prettier rolls, smooth and reshape each one as you lay it on the baking sheet. Let rolls rise at room temperature until puffy and light, about one hour. Rolls can be brushed with melted butter before or after baking. Bake in upper third of oven at 400°F about 10 minutes. Makes 30 rolls.

NOTE: I reheat rolls the way my grandmother did ... in a paper bag, sprinkled with a little water and folded securely at the top. Place bag in middle of a 350°F oven for 10 to 15 minutes.

Crescent Rolls

One of the most popular ways of shaping yeast rolls . . .

Rich Yeast Dough, page 128
1/2 cup (1 cube) butter, melted

Prepare yeast dough. Chill it immediately. Divide chilled dough into thirds. Roll out one third into a 12-inch circle. Refrigerated the rest until needed. Spread generously with melted butter. Cut into 12 pie-shaped wedges. Roll each wedge up, starting at the wide end. (It is all right to stretch dough a little as you roll it firmly.) Place point down on a baking sheet. Stretch in the middle, and curve the ends into a crescent. Repeat with the other two pieces of dough. Brush tops of rolls with melted butter, if desired. Cover lightly with plastic or a dish towel (not terrycloth). Let rise about 3 hours at room temperature. (The chilled dough takes longer to rise.) Bake at 400°F in the upper third of oven for 8 to 10 minutes. Makes 36 rolls.

Cinnamon Raisin Nut Bread

Rich Yeast Dough, page 128
1/3 cup raisins
1/4 cup walnuts or pecans
3 tbs. sugar
1 tsp. cinnamon

Grease two 4 x 8-inch or 3-1/2 x 9-inch loaf pans. Pat or roll dough into rectangle 16 to 18 inches long and about 8 inches wide. (If dough resists, let is rest awhile.) Sprinkle on raisins and nuts. Continue shaping the rectangle, pressing in nuts and raisins as you go. Dip hand in cold water and moisten surface of dough. Combine sugar and cinnamon and sprinkle over moistened surface. Roll dough tightly, starting with a small fold along the long edge. Stretch dough a little as you roll it like a jelly roll. Pinch far edges to seal. With side of hand give a firm downward motion to separate into two loaves. Tuck other ends under and place in greased pans. Let rise, covered with dish towel, about 1-1/2 hours. Spear 5 or 6 times through risen loaves with moistened skewer or trussing needle to collapse any large air spaces. Bake in lower third of 375°F oven 30 minutes. Makes 2 loaves.

Danish Sweet Rolls

Rich Yeast Dough, page 128
1 cup (2 cubes) butter, frozen
2/3 cup red raspberry or apricot jam
Glaze, page 133

Prepare yeast dough. (If a sweeter dough is desired, increase sugar to 1/2 cup.) Using **slicing disc,** cut frozen butter into slivers. Fold into soft dough. Cover and chill. Work with one third of dough at a time. Refrigerate remainder. Roll dough into a 1/2-inch-thick rectangle 5 inches wide by 10 inches long. Cut crosswise into one-inch strips. (Use a large chef's knife, so one downward motion cuts each piece off.) Twist strips one at a time, by placing palm of one hand lightly on one end of strip while holding the opposite end with your other hand. Twist strip toward yourself. Pick up both ends, and tie a knot. One end comes up through center, while the other end is tucked under roll. Arrange rolls on ungreased baking sheet. Repeat with remaining dough. Let rise until doubled in size, about two hours. Make a depression in the center of each roll. Fill with a teaspoon of jam. Bake in 100°F oven 8 to 10 minutes. Glaze rolls while warm, or later, if desired. Makes 30 small rolls.

GLAZE

2 cups powdered sugar
2 to 3 tbs. cream
1/2 tsp. vanilla or almond extract

Using **steel blade,** process ingredients until blended. Spread on rolls.

Variation:
Figure 8's: Cut and twist strips of dough as for Danish Rolls. Instead of forming a knot, bring both ends of twisted strip together, allowing the loop to dangle. It will twist itself into a figure 8. Tuck ends under. Allow to rise at room temperature until puffy and doubled in size, about two hours. Place jelly inside each loop. Two different flavors in one roll looks pretty. Bake in 400°F oven 8 to 10 minutes. Glaze and sprinkle with chopped or sliced almonds. Makes 30 Figure 8's.

Small Chocolate-Filled Rolls

These rolls are popular in France ... in fact, they are popular with everyone I know who has tasted them!

Rich Yeast Dough, page 128
1 4-oz. bar semi-sweet chocolate
Browned Butter Icing, page 135
1/4 cup chocolate sprinkles
or 1/3 cup toasted almonds, slivered, sliced or chopped

Prepare yeast dough. Cover lightly with waxed paper or plastic. Let rise 1-1/2 to 2 hours at room temperature. When dough has risen to double its original volume, turn out onto generously floured surface. Pat lightly with floured hands (or use a very light touch on a floured rolling pin) to a thickness of one-half inch. Cut rolls with a 2-1/2-inch round cutter. Divide chocolate bar into 30 pieces ... one per roll. (I try to make the pieces 1/2 x 1-1/4-inch.) Shape each circle of dough around a piece of chocolate. Pinch the edges together, making an oval or football shape. (To accomplish this I cradle the roll in the palm of one hand while using the side of my other hand to seal the dough around the chocolate and ease it into the oval shape.) Place rolls on ungreased baking sheets about 2 inches apart. Let rise until puffy and nearly double in size. Rolls will be ready to bake when a small depression remains after touching lightly with a finger. Bake in upper third of a 400°F oven 8 to 10 minutes. Cool. Spread with icing and garnish with chocolate sprinkles or almonds. Makes 30 rolls.

BROWNED BUTTER ICING

4 tbs. butter
2-1/2 cups powdered sugar
1/2 tsp. vanilla
2 tbs. cream (approximately)

Carefully heat butter until it is light brown. (Watch closely; it burns easily.) Add powdered sugar and vanilla. Blend in enough cream to make a spreading consistency. Makes enough for 30 rolls.

Clarice's Brown Bread

My sister who lives in Iowa has shared many recipes from "Heartland, USA." I adapted her bread recipe to the food processor and gained all the rewards of homemade bread in less than the usual time.

2/3 cup very warm (105°-115°) water
1 tbs. sugar
1 pkg. (1 tbs.) active dry yeast
1-1/2 cups white flour
1-1/2 cups whole wheat flour

2 tbs. brown sugar, honey or molasses
3 tbs. butter, margarine, shortening or oil
1 tsp. salt
1 cup undiluted evaporated milk
1/2 cup white or wheat flour for kneading

Combine water, sugar and yeast in a 2 cup measure. Stir and set aside. With **steel blade** inserted in food processor bowl, add white and whole wheat flour, brown sugar, butter and salt. If butter is firm, process a few seconds to cut in into the flour. Pour in yeast mixture and half the lukewarm milk. Start processor. Immediately add remaining evaporated milk through the feed tube. Stop processor when mixture forms a ball . . . this will be almost simultaneous with the addition of the last of the milk. There may be a slowing of the blades. Stop immediately if you detect this. Sprinkle half of the kneading flour on a smooth surface. Turn dough out of bowl onto flour using a rubber scraper if necessary to remove all of dough. Sprinkle with part of remaining flour. Let dough rest a minute while you grease two tall 1-pound cans with 1/2 tablespoon shortening each. Using a pastry scraper and a gentle touch, turn the dough in kneading motions, gradually using your hands instead of the pastry scraper. It takes only 2 to 3 minutes for this dough to become smooth and elastic. The half cup flour should be sufficient. Squeeze to divide dough into two equal balls. Drop into prepared cans. Rap cans sharply to help dough settle into cans. Let rise in warm place 1 or 2 hours. Place rack in lower third of oven. Turn oven on to 350°F when dough is level with tops of cans. Bake bread 45 minutes. Lift loaves from cans immediately upon removal from oven. If they don't come out easily, wait about 5 minutes. Cool on racks. Makes 2 tall mushroom shaped loaves.

NOTE: To slice a mushroom shaped loaf of bread, lay loaf on its side and slice in rounds from the bottom to just below the "bulge." Then turn remaining rounded top of loaf, cut side down, and slice vertically like a mushroom.

Rich No-Knead Yeast Loaves

They taste almost like brioche. Great for toasting when a day or two old.

1 cube (1/4 lb.) margarine
1/2 cup milk
2/3 cup very warm tap water
1 tsp. sugar
1 pkg. active dry yeast

3 cups flour
1/4 cup sugar
1 tsp. salt
2 eggs

Generously grease two 1-pound coffee cans or 3 x 9-inch loaf pans. Set aside. Cut margarine in several slices. Heat with milk until nearly melted. Set aside. Combine very warm water, 1 teaspoon sugar and the yeast. Stir until blended and set aside. Insert **steel blade** in food processor bowl. Add flour, 1/4 cup sugar, eggs, and yeast mixture. Process until blended. For more convenient pouring through feed tube, transfer hot milk mixture to a measuring cup with pouring lip. With processor running, pour in milk. Turn processor off immediately. Scrape sides. Process another few seconds. Pour batter into prepared cans. Let rise until double in size and level with top of cans. Bake in lower third of 375°F oven 35 minutes. Turn out of cans. Cool on racks. Makes 2 loaves.

Danish Coffee Cake

A variation of Rich No-Knead Dough (page 138) that tastes like the coffee cake my grandmother used to make.

5 cardamom pods, crushed
or 1/4 tsp. ground cardamom
1/3 cup raisins or currants

1 tbs. melted butter
2 tbs. sugar
1 tsp. cinnamon

Add cardamom to flour called for in the recipe for Rich No-Knead Yeast Loaves on page 138. When dough is all mixed and after scraping sides of processor bowl, add raisins just before final few seconds of processing. Brush bottom and sides of a 7 x 11-inch or 9 x 9-inch pan with some of the melted butter. Pour in batter. Flatten top with scraper. Dribble on remaining butter. Combine sugar and cinnamon. Sprinkle heavily over top of batter. Let rise until double in volume. Bake on middle rack of 375°F oven 35 minutes. Cool in pan on cake rack. To serve, cut down middle with serrated knife. Then cut crosswise in 3/4-inch slices. Makes 10 to 12 servings of two slices each.

Pizza Crust

Can be made, shaped and partially baked hours ahead.

2-1/2 cups flour
1 tsp. salt
3 tsp. oil
1 cup hot tap water
1 tsp. <u>each</u> dry yeast and sugar

Insert **steel blade** in processor bowl. Measure 1-1/2 cups flour into bowl. Add salt and 1 teaspoon oil to flour. Combine water, yeast and sugar in measuring cup with pouring lip. With processor running, add liquid mixture through feed tube. Process about one minute. Add 1/2 cup more flour. Process with one or two "on-off" turns. Sprinkle remaining half cup flour on smooth surface. Place 1 teaspoon oil in a deep, 1-1/2 quart bowl. Turn dough onto floured surface. Knead using as much of the flour as necessary to make a smooth, elastic ball. Dip into oil in bowl and turn to grease all sides. Cover with plastic wrap. Let rise about one hour. During this time prepare sauce, cheese and toppings. Brush 1 teaspoon oil on 13 x 17-inch rimmed baking sheet or 2 pizza pans. Turn dough out onto baking sheet. Press gently but firmly with oiled hands, working dough gradually to sides of pan. If dough is reluctant to stretch, let it rest a while. Then continue distributing it evenly in pan. Try to avoid tearing as holes are nearly impossible to patch. Pre-bake crust immediately for thin crust or after a rest of about 20 minutes if you like a little thicker and less crispy crust. Bake in lower third of 400°F oven 10 minutes. Crust should be set but not very brown when removed from oven. This can be done early in the day.

Cakes and Quick Breads

With the aid of a food processor, "scratch" cakes and quick breads can be mixed almost as quickly as those from mixes.

The procedure for preparing a cake mix with the food processor differs somewhat from the package directions. Combine cake mix, eggs and only 1/3 cup of the water called for, in processor bowl. Process, using **steel blade,** just long enough to blend. Add remaining water through the feed tube. Process until smooth and fluffy, about one minute. Pour into prepared pans and bake as directed.

Cornbread and other quick breads can also be mixed successfully. Instead of melting the shortening, cut it into the dry ingredients. (It's easier and saves having an extra pan to wash). Liquid is added last and very quickly. Turn processor off as soon as all liquid is added to avoid overmixing.

Lemon Loaf Cake

A tender delicate pound cake that that can be thinly sliced to serve with tea or to accompany fresh fruit or berries for a delightful summertime dessert.

2 cups cake flour (sift before measuring)
1-1/2 cup sugar
1/2 tsp. salt
4 thin strips (1/2 x 2 in.) lemon zest
1 tbs. lemon juice
1 tsp. vanilla
1/2 cup (1 cube) butter, cut in 5 or 6 pieces
1/2 cup vegetable shortening
5 eggs

Grease the ends of a 5 x 9-inch loaf pan. Line the sides and bottom with waxed paper or baking parchment. Insert **steel blade** in food processor bowl. Add flour, sugar, salt, strips of lemon zest (removed with vegetable peeler), lemon juice, vanilla, butter and shortening. Break eggs into a two-cup measure. Turn on processor for about 20

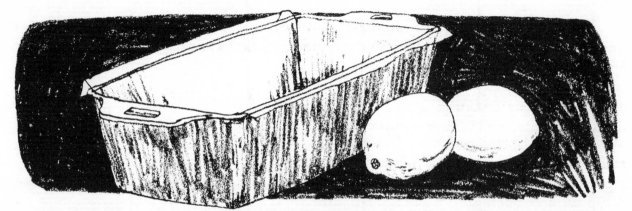

seconds, until butter and lemon zest are finely cut into other ingredients. With processor still running, add eggs through the feed tube, one after another. When batter is smooth, turn into prepared pan. Bake in lower middle of a 325°F oven for one hour and 20 minutes. If top becomes too brown, protect it with a "tent" of foil or brown paper. Cake will shrink from pan and feel dry on the top when it is done. Let cool a few minutes, then turn out on cake rack to cool completely. Wrap in plastic or put into a plastic bag for continued storage. Cake slices better the day after it is baked.

Bourbon-Nut Poundcake

A lovely flavored and fine textured cake that keeps well. It can be wrapped in a bourbon-soaked cloth to inhance its flavor and extend its keeping qualities. Serve thinly sliced with vanilla or coffee ice cream.

1 cup walnuts or pecans
2 cups cake flour (sift before measuring)
1/2 tsp. <u>each</u> baking powder and salt
1/2 tsp. <u>each</u> cinnamon and nutmeg
1 cup (2 cubes) butter
1 cup sugar
1/4 cup bourbon
4 eggs <u>plus</u> 1 yolk

Grease a 5 x 9-inch loaf pan with 1 tablespoon soft shortening. Line pan with double waxed paper or baking parchment. Insert **steel blade** in food processor bowl. Add nuts, flour, baking powder, salt, cinnamon and nutmeg. Cut each cube of butter into 5 or 6 pieces. Add to bowl along with sugar and bourbon. Break eggs into a measuring cup with pouring lip. Add extra yolk to make a total of one cup. (If using extra-large eggs the extra yolk may be unnecessary.) Turn on processor for 10 to 15 seconds. When the butter and nuts are cut finely you will notice a smooth sound. Add the eggs through the feed tube with processor running. By the time the last egg slips in, the mixture should be smooth. Turn into prepared pan. Cover loosely with a hood made from a brown paper bag or baking parchment. (Remove after 40 minutes.) Bake cake in the middle of a 325°F oven for 1 hour and 15 minutes, or until cake shrinks slightly from sides of pan. Remove from oven and cool on cake rack. Cake slices best after 24 hours. For longer storage soak cheese cloth with about 1/3 cup bourbon and wrap cake tightly. Follow with a wrapping of foil. Store in an airtight container. Makes 1 loaf.

Cranberry Cake
with Vanilla Butter Sauce

It's worth keeping cranberries in the freezer just for this cake!

1 cup fresh cranberries
1/4 cup walnuts or pecans
2 tbs. butter
1/2 cup sugar
1 cup flour

1/2 tsp. salt
1 tsp. baking soda
1/4 cup evaporated milk
1/4 cup water

Using **steel blade**, chop cranberries coarsly. Pour into medium-size mixing bowl. Chop nuts coarsely. Add to cranberries. Measure butter into a 9 x 9- inch or 7 x 11-inch pan. Place in oven so butter will melt as oven preheats to 350°F. Remove pan when butter is melted. Tilt pan to butter sides and bottom. Without washing processor bowl continue with **steel blade,** or switch to plastic blade. Add sugar, melted butter, flour, salt and soda. Process to blend. Combine evaporated milk and water. Add to dry ingredients. Blend again with one or two quick "on-off" turns. Turn batter into bowl with cranberries and nuts. Stir to blend evenly. Pour into buttered pan. Bake at 350°F for 25 minutes. Serve with Vanilla Butter Sauce. Makes 8 or 9 servings.

VANILLA BUTTER SAUCE

Delicious on cranberry cake, steamed puddings, and bread pudding.

1 cup sugar
4 tbs. butter
1/2 cup evaporated milk
1 tsp. vanilla

Combine sugar, butter, and evaporated milk in heavy saucepan. Stir over medium-high heat until mixture comes to a boil. Continue cooking, while stirring constantly, for 5 minutes. Remove from heat, and add vanilla. Serve warm. Makes 8 or 9 generous servings.

Variations:
Brandy Butter Sauce—Use 1 tablespoon of brandy and 1/2 tsp. vanilla.
Rum Butter Sauce—Use 1 to 2 tablespoons rum instead of vanilla.

Gingerbread

Serve with whipped cream or Apricot Rum Sauce (page 151) . . . or both!

1-1/4 cups flour	1 tsp. cinnamon
3/4 tsp. baking soda	1 egg
1/2 tsp. salt	1/3 cup salad oil
1/4 cup sugar	1/3 cup molasses
1 tsp. ginger	1/2 cup boiling water

Grease the ends of two 3 x 6-inch pans using 1 to 2 teaspoons shortening. Line bottom and sides with waxed paper or baking parchment. Insert **steel blade** in food processor bowl. Add flour, soda, salt, sugar, ginger and cinnamon. Hold hand over feed tube and process a few seconds to blend. Remove cover. Add egg, oil and molasses. Blend a few seconds. Stop and pour in boiling water. Blend again with only an "off-on." Pour into prepared pans. Bake in 350°F oven 30 to 35 minutes, or until gingerbread shrinks slightly from ends of pans and feels dry on top. Makes 2 loaves which can be sliced into 10 dessert servings.

Apricot Rum Sauce

Serve over gingerbread, or fill crepes with vanilla ice cream, roll and spoon warm sauce over top.

1 cup apricot jam	2 strips (1/2 x 2-in.) orange zest
1/3 cup water	3 to 4 tbs. rum
2 tbs. sugar	1/4 cup chopped walnuts or toasted slivered almonds

Warm apricot jam and water in small saucepan. With **steel blade** inserted process sugar and orange zest until sugar takes on an orange color and zest is finely chopped. Stir into jam and water. Boil 2 to 3 minutes. If a smoother sauce is desired, process with **steel blade** until smooth. Blend in rum and nuts. Makes enough for about 10 servings.

Variation:

Orange Walnut Sauce—Substitute orange marmelade for apricot jam. Add Cointreau or Triple Sec instead of rum. Flame with 3 tablespoons Grand Marnier or brandy.

Banana Squash Bread

In winter, when banana squash is inexpensive, I serve it often and always cook extra to make this spicy bread. It is also delicious made with pumpkin. Serve warm with butter or with Whipped Cream Cheese (page 40).

1-1/4 cups cooked banana squash
2 eggs
1/2 cup vegetable oil
1 cup brown sugar
2 cups flour
1/2 tsp. baking powder
1/2 tsp. each salt and soda

1 tsp. cinnamon
1 tsp. ginger, optional
1 or 2 cardamom pods
or 1/8 tsp. ground cardamom
1 tsp. vanilla
1/2 cup chopped walnuts or pecans
1/2 cup dates, pitted and halved

Grease the ends of two 3-1/2 x 7-inch or one 5 x 9-inch loaf pan well. Line sides and bottoms with waxed paper or baking parchment. Set aside. Using **steel blade,** puree squash. Add eggs, oil, and sugar. Process a few seconds to blend. Measure flour into sifter. Add baking powder, salt, soda, cinnamon and ginger. Sift into squash mixture. Remove cardamom seeds from pods and crush. Add crushed cardamom and vanilla to mixture. Process just until blended. Add nuts and dates. Mix through batter gently with rubber scraper. Turn batter into prepared pans. Smooth tops. Rap each pan sharply to jar out air spaces. Bake at a middle level of a 325°F oven for 1 hour and 15 minutes, or until bread pulls away from pan slightly. Loosen ends, and turn out on racks to cool. Makes 2 small loaves or one 5 x 9 loaf.

NOTE: If you find yourself short of cooked squash, complete the measure with yogurt of buttermilk.

Creative Returns

Stretching the imagination and the budget along with it, is a reality when a food processor sits available for use. Because it handles small amounts perfectly, seldom is an idea rejected by the thought "Will it be worth it?" Yes, it will be worth it. Pizza for dinner might result from a piece of Canadian bacon no larger than half an apple, and "end" of salami, a few mushrooms, a bit of onion, and assorted cheese (each item sliced, chopped or shredded in seconds with the food processor) and a little pizza sauce, made ahead and in the freezer, ready and waiting. Crepes are another favorite way of making something terrific out of almost nothing. For real fun, see Stacked Crepes in this section, or consider cannelloni. Chop bits of leftover meat, mushrooms and spinach. Wrap in crepes and place in a shallow baking dish. Pour Tomato Herb Sauce (page 74) and/or Mornay Sauce (page 9) over the top and sprinkle with shredded cheese. Heat thoroughly and serve with pride.

Don't hesitate to try new ideas ... you can depend on your food processor to make it easy and fun. Learn to enjoy the challenge of providing exciting meals from "a little of this and a little of that." It's a great outlet for your creativity!

Food Processor Crepes

Crepes are a marvelous way to present leftovers. Bits and pieces of meat, chicken, seafood or vegetables can be combined with a Mornay or curry sauce, rolled in crepes and served in a most elegant manner. A food processor is so efficient at chopping meat, or slicing mushrooms, or pureeing vegetables, it's easy to create a delicious filling from the "treasures" you'll find hidden in your refrigerator. Try it and see! This crepe batter can be used immmediately, however the crepes will be more tender if it rests an hour or so.

1 cup flour
2 tbs. butter
1/4 to 1/2 tsp. salt
2 eggs
1/3 cup water
1 cup milk
oil for frying

Insert **steel blade** into food processor bowl. Add flour, butter and salt. Process a few seconds until butter is finely cut into flour. Add eggs and water. With processor running, add milk through feed tube. Process until blended. To bake crepes quickly, use 2 or 3 pans. Two should be the same size, 6 inches, and the third the same or larger. Heat over medium to medium-high heat. Add about 1/2 teaspoon oil. Crepes can be cooked without adding oil to the pan each time, but they are more lacy if you do. For easy pouring transfer crepe batter to a quart measure. Drops of water will dance on a properly heated pan. Pour about 2 tablespoons batter into hot pan. Rotate pan quickly, and empty any batter not needed to coat bottom of pan back into container. Pour batter into second pan in like manner. When first crepe shows browning at the edges, transfer to third pan for cooking second side. Add oil and batter to first pan as before. Remove crepe from third pan, put crepe from second pan into third pan. Repeat until all batter is used. It only takes a little practice and you'll love being able to bake crepes so quickly. When you've mastered three pans, try four! To store crepes, cool at room temperature. Stack without anything between them. Store in stacks of 8, 10, or 12, whatever you'll most likely need. Wrap in plastic or foil. They keep five days in the refrigerator. Freeze for longer storage. Reheat when needed in 375°F oven or on warming tray until soft. Makes 18 to 20 six-inch crepes.

Ham Filled Crepes

18 six-inch crepes, page 156
4 cups milk
6 tbs. (3/4 cube) butter
1/2 cup flour
3/4 tsp. salt
freshly ground white pepper

freshly grated nutmeg
4 cups cooked ham cubes or chunks
1 red bell pepper or a few
  pimiento stuffed green olives
1 tbs. butter

Bake or defrost crepes. Heat milk. Melt butter in top of double boiler over direct heat. Add flour and cook, stirring, 3 to 4 minutes. Remove from heat. Whisk in boiling milk. Add salt, pepper and nutmeg. Cover and cook over simmering water half an hour. Stir once or twice. With **steel blade** inserted in food processor bowl, chop ham coarsely in two or three batches. Transfer to a bowl as chopping is completed. Cut pepper in quarters. Remove seeds and cut each quarter in 2 or 3 pieces. Saute in butter 5 minutes. Mix with ham. (If using olives cut in half and omit sauteeing.) Add about half of the sauce to ham. Stir gently to combine. Place a large tablespoon of filling on each crepe. Roll and place side-by-side in lightly buttered, oven-to-table dish or individual au gratin dishes. Spoon remaining sauce over crepes. Don't hide the crepes by covering them completely. Heat in upper third of 375°F oven until sauce is bubbly, 20 to 25 minutes. Makes 6 servings of 3 crepes each.

 ## Stacked Crepes

Make crepes thicker for this dish. Then assemble by stacking crepes flat with assorted and varied fillings between layers. For the fillings, coarsely chop leftover cooked meat, chicken, seafood or vegetables using the **steel blade.** Combine with enough well-seasoned sauce, such as Mornay or Tomato Herb to give a desired consistency. Spread fillings (a different one for each layer, if desired) between crepes. Stack about 2 inches high. Cover with sauce and sprinkle with shredded cheese. Heat in 350°F oven about 30 to 35 minutes, until warmed through and sauce is bubbly and browned on top. Cut in wedges to serve. Eight-inch crepes stacked 2 inches high, will make 4 to 6 servings. Serve as a first course for dinner, or as a brunch or luncheon dish.

Fish Patties with Dill Sauce

It's economical to cook extra fish so there will be enough left to make this recipe. Serve with stewed tomatoes and mashed potatoes.

20 2-inch saltines (1 cup crushed)
3 sprigs parsley
1/2 cup milk
1/2 medium onion, cut in chunks
1/2 green pepper, cut in chunks
1-1/2 to 2 cups flaked albacore*
1 egg
1/2 to 1 tsp. salt
2 to 3 tbs. oil
Dill Sauce, page 162

Insert **steel blade** in food processor bowl. Turn on processor and drop saltines through feed tube. Hold your hand over the opening to prevent crumbs from flying out. Cut parsley and stems into one-inch pieces. Drop in with crumbs. Process until finely chopped. Turn into a medium-size bowl. Add milk. Stir to moisten crumbs. Reassemble **steel blade** in bowl. Process onion and green pepper until chopped. Transfer to bowl with crumbs. Carefully check fish for bones you may be missed. (If using canned fish, drain it well.) Still using **steel blade,** process fish into medium-size flakes. Remove to bowl of crumbs. Add egg (or two egg whites if you have them left after making Hollandaise for baked fish, or a thick mayonnaise), pepper and salt. Stir to blend. Add more salt if needed. Heat oil in a large skillet over medium heat. Carefully drop rounded tablespoonfuls of hot fish mixture into hot fat. Turn when brown and cook on the other side. It takes about 5 minutes on each side. Patties can be held in skillet for about 20 minutes by turning heat very low when cooking the second side. Or, they can be removed to serving platter and kept warm in 150°F oven. Garnish with parsley sprigs and lemon wedges. Serve with Dill Sauce. Makes 5 or 6 servings of 2 patties each.

*or other cooked fish (1 pound before cooking). 2 cans (6-7 ozs. ea.) albacore, tuna or a l-pound can salmon.

DILL SAUCE

1-1/2 tbs. butter
2 tbs. flour
1-1/4 cups milk, heated
1/2 tsp. salt
freshly ground white pepper
freshly ground nutmeg
1/8 tsp. dried dill weed
1/4 cup sour cream
1 to 2 tsp. lemon juice, optional

Melt butter in small heavy saucepan or double boiler. Add flour and cook 2 minutes. Whisk in heated milk. Add salt, pepper, nutmeg and dill. Cook at least five minutes or as long as 30 minutes. Just before serving stir in sour cream and lemon juice, if used. Reheat gently but it won't be ruined if it boils! Makes about 1-3/4 cups. Serve with patties or any simply baked, broiled or poached fish.

Roast Beef Hash Danish-Style

This is my grandmother's recipe. Serve with cole slaw, sliced tomatoes and Fresh Pickle Slices (page 43). Fruit pudding goes well for dessert.

2 to 3 slices day-old bread
3 tbs. butter
2 cups leftover roast beef pieces
4 medium russet potatoes, peeled
1 onion

1 tsp. salt
1/4 tsp. pepper
2 cups gravy, meat juices, broth,
    water or a combination, warmed

Tear bread slices in quarters. Using **steel blade** make buttered crumbs of torn bread and 2 tablespoon butter. Set aside. Use remaining butter to grease an 8 by 12-inch casserole. Cut beef (or pork) chunks, potatoes and onion in 1-inch pieces. Without washing bowl and still using **steel blade,** process meat, potatoes and onion in two cup amounts until medium fine. Combine all in the buttered casserole. Add salt and pepper. Pour liquid over hash mixture. Stir lightly. Sprinkle with buttered crumbs. Bake in 375°F oven 45 to 50 minutes. Makes 6 servings.

New Horizons

I encourage you to try the recipes in this section, as well as other different and interesting ones. Look for glamorous new ideas where the food processor can work its magic and make once difficult chores easier. Perhaps there is a particular dish you enjoyed at a fine restaurant and would like to serve to guests. Gather your courage and try it soon.

Many elegant dishes can, or must, be prepared in advance, leaving you free to enjoy your own party and guests. Your choice is unlimited even if your time is not.

The food processor has changed "life in the kitchen" and has opened up new horizons and added even more excitement to cooking and dining.

Quenelles of Sole

1/2 recipe Pâte à Choux, page 106
3/4 lb. filets of sole
1 egg white
1/2 tsp. salt
1/4 tsp. white pepper

1/4 tsp. nutmeg
1/4 to 1/3 cup heavy cream
2 qts. simmering water
2 tsp. salt
Shrimp Sauce, page 167

Cut the recipe for pâte à choux, on page 106, in half (or make a full recipe as directed. Use half in this recipe, and make cream puffs with the remainder). Cover pâte à choux (1/2 recipe) and chill. Cut filets into pieces. Place in processor bowl with **steel blade** inserted. Add salt, pepper and nutmeg. Process until puréed. Add egg white through feed tube and blend in. Add chilled pâte à choux. Slowly add cream through the feed tube and blend in. Refrigerate mixture until ready to poach quenelles. Have water with salt barely simmering in a large skillet or pan. Shape rounded teaspoonfuls of quenelle mixture and slip into water. Cook about 12 to 15 minutes. Carefully lift from water and drain. Serve with Shrimp Sauce.

SHRIMP SAUCE

2 cups milk	1/2 tsp. salt	1 tsp. tomato paste
3 tbs. butter	freshly ground white pepper	1/4 cup heavy cream
1/4 cup flour	freshly grated nutmeg	1 cup cooked shrimp

Heat milk. Melt butter in top of double boiler. Blend in flour. When milk is boiling whisk it into butter-flour mixture. Add salt, pepper and nutmeg. Scrape sides. Cover and cook over hot water about 1/2 hour. Just before serving add tomato paste, cream and shrimp. Serve over quenelles.

Variations:

Add 1 tablespoon dry sherry to sauce.

For a smooth sauce puree shrimp with 1 tablespoon butter using **steel blade.** Process until extremely smooth. Blend into sauce

For a very special occasion, sprinkle Quenelles of Sole with 1 tablespoon chopped truffles. Add truffle juice to the sauce.

Chicken Breast Mousse with Cream Sauce

1/2 recipe Pâte à Choux, page 106
2-1/2 lbs. chicken breasts
1-1/4 tsp. salt
1/4 tsp. white pepper
1/4 tsp. nutmeg
2 tbs. cognac

1 cup (7 to 8 large) egg whites
1-1/2 cubes butter, softened
1-1/2 cups heavy cream
14 1/2-cup dariole molds or custard cups
Cream Sauce, page 169

Cut the recipe for pâte à choux, on page 106 in half (or make a full recipe as directed. Use half in this recipe and make cream puffs with the remainder). Chill pâte à choux (1/2 recipe). Skin and bone chicken breasts. Cut into pieces to make 3 cups. Puree chicken and seasonings in processor bowl fitted with the **steel blade.** Add egg whites through the feed tube with the processor running. Add chilled pâte à choux and then butter, barely blending each. Slowly add cream through the feed tube until mixture is very fluffy, yet holds it shape. Spoon mixture into buttered dariole molds or custard cups. Give each a sharp rap to force out air bubbles. Set in a large skillet which has a lid. Surround with boiling water. Cover with buttered waxed paper and the lid. Simmer 15 minutes. Remove from heat. Keep warm in same water and pan until ready to serve. Unmold and serve with Cream Sauce. Makes 14 first course or 7 main course servings.

CREAM SAUCE

1-1/4 cups chicken broth
3 tbs. butter
4-1/2 tbs. flour
1/2 tsp. paprika
salt and white pepper
1/2 cup heavy cream
truffles, optional

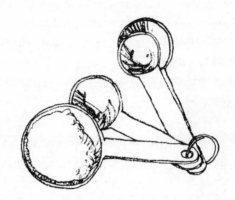

    Heat broth. Melt butter and stir in flour. Cook together 2 minutes. Add hot broth, paprika, salt and pepper. Just before serving, whip cream and fold into hot sauce. Spoon over mousse. Scatter a few chopped truffles on top to be really fancy!

Creme Calcutta

Terrific! Serve with chicken salad and hot rolls or French bread.

3 cans (10-3/4 ozs.) double-
   strength chicken broth
1 qt. water
1/2 cup uncooked rice
4 large onions

4 tbs. (1/2 cube) butter
3 tsp. curry powder
1 cup light or heavy cream
chopped parsley, tarragon,
   chopped cashews or toasted coconut

Heat chicken broth and water in a 4-quart pot. When boiling, stir in rice. Cook 20 minutes. Peel onions, and cut into chunks. Using **steel blade,** chop onions in two or three batches. Melt butter in large skillet. Add onion, and cook over medium heat until transparent. Stir occasionally. Do not allow to brown. Add curry powder. Cook 10 minutes longer. When onions are soft and a rich yellow color, add to rice mixture. Cook together 20 minutes longer. Using **steel blade** process warm soup, 2 cups at a time, until pureed. Just before serving, add cream. Serve garnished with parsley, tarragon, and a sprinkling of cashews or coconut. Makes 8 generous servings.

Chef Narces' Bearnaise Sauce

If you have mastered the technique of making Hollandaise (page 52) add this to your accomplishments.

1 handful fresh tarragon*	1 cube (1/2 cup) butter	freshly grated nutmeg
2 shallots, halved	2 tbs. cold water	1 tsp. chopped fresh
2 tbs. white wine vingar	2 egg yolks	tarragon and parsley
freshly ground pepper	1/8 tsp. salt	

Finely chop tarragon leaves with sharp knife (about 1 tablespoon). With **steel blade** in motion, drop shallots through feed tube. Combine tarragon, shallots, vinegar and pepper. Boil until nearly all liquid is evaporated. Watch carefully. Cool. Melt butter. Add cold water to tarragon mixture. Add egg yolks. Whisk briskly over medium heat until thickened and fluffy (sabayon stage). Cool until same temperature as butter and you can touch the sides of both pans without burning hands. Quickly whisk warm butter into sabayon. Add salt if needed, nutmeg and a little pepper. Sprinkle with herbs. Makes 3/4 cup.
*2 teaspoons dried tarragon and 1 tablespoon chopped fresh parsley.

Braised Lettuce

Here is a truly different and elegent vegetable dish. In France Braised Lettuce is a typical accompaniment for veal or lamb.

6 qts. water
6 heads butter lettuce or small romaine
2 tbs. salt
Mirepoix: 1/2 large onion
        1 medium carrot
        1 small rib celery
        2 or 3 slices bacon
        6 parsley stems (no leaves)
        1/4 tsp. salt

3 to 4 tbs. butter
1/2 tsp. salt
1/4 cup cream sherry
1/4 tsp. pepper
1/4 tsp. nutmeg
2 sprigs fresh thyme
1 bay leaf

Bring water to boil in a large pot. Wash lettuce well. Split in half vertically. Trim bases slightly. Keep enough of the stem to hold leaves together. Plunge lettuce into rapidly boiling water. Add salt after boiling resumes. Boil 8 to 10 minutes, until stalk is

tender. Drain and place in colander to drain. <u>To prepare mirepoix</u>, cut onion, carrot and celery into chunks. Fit **steel blade** into food processor bowl. Process onion, carrot, celery and bacon until all are finely chopped. Chop parsley stems with a sharp knife. Turn all into a medium-size, non-stick skillet. Cook over medium-low heat about 10 minutes. Stir occasionally. Do not allow to brown. Add salt. Spread mirepoix in bottom of a shallow oven-to-table dish. Squeeze and press as much water from lettuce as possible. Fold limp upper leaves back over cut slices toward base. Squeeze again. Lettuce halves will be in a flattened fan shape at this point. Melt butter in large frying pan. Brown lettuce on both sides over medium-high heat. Season generously with salt, pepper and nutmeg. Arrange lettuce over mirepoix, overlapping if necessary to make all fit. Deglaze skillet with sherry. Pour sherry juices over lettuce. Lay thyme sprigs (or 1/8 teaspoon dried thyme leaves) and bay leaf on top. Cover with a piece of buttered waxed paper and then foil. Braise in 375°F oven 35 to 45 minutes. The lettuce should remain moist, with most of the sherry absorbed or evaporated. Remove thyme and bay leaf before serving. Makes 6 generous servings.
NOTE: Mirepoix is a classic base of aromatic vegetables and herbs. It is one of the foundation stones of French cooking.

Poached Eggs Ostendaise

Consider this for your most appreciative gourmet friends. Poached eggs in tartelette shells with a rich shrimp sauce makes a superb first couse for a dinner, or is impressive for brunch served with a butter lettuce salad, dressed with olive oil and lemon juice, and a fresh fruit tray. Every part of this dish can be prepared ahead leaving only the "putting together" for the last minute.

12 baked tartelette shells, page 96
12 poached eggs, page 175
Rich Shrimp Sauce, page 177
Hollandaise Sauce, page 52
1 black truffle or 12 black olive halves
12 small parsley sprigs

Make tartelette shells as directed. These can be made days in advance and frozen. Bake early in the day. Poach eggs and hold in water as directed. Make both sauces in advance and slice truffle into 12 thin slices. Just before serving, warm tartelettes. Have Rich Shrimp Sauce hot in double boiler. Hollandaise should be at room temperature and eggs warming in hot water. When ready to serve, stir one spoonful Rich Shrimp Sauce into Hollandaise. Then stir in two or three more to equalize the temperature of the two sauces. Now fold all of the remaining Rich Shrimp Sauce into Hollandaise. Drain warmed eggs on towel. Lay one egg in each tartelette shell. Spoon sauce generously over eggs. Top each with a truffle slice or olive half. Lay a sprig of parsley beside each. Serve individually on warm plates or arrange all on a warm tray or platter. Makes 12 servings. This is truly haute cuisine!

POACHED EGGS

2 qts. water
1/2 cup white vinegar
12 eggs

Combine water and vinegar in large, 2-inch deep skillet. Heat to simmering. Stir water to make a swirl. Carefully break each egg and while holding very close to water slip egg out of shell into skillet. The first one goes into small whirlpool in the center. The

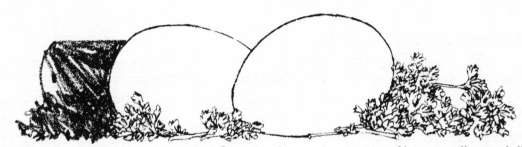

rest should be slipped in around it. Poach about 4 minutes. If you will carefully nudge the eggs with a spatula so they are loose from the bottom of the pan, they will rise to the surface when the white is sufficiently set, about 4 minutes. Remove from pan with slotted spoon, starting with the first egg added to the water. Drain eggs on folded dish towel to absorb moisture before serving.

NOTE: Eggs can be poached several hours or even a day ahead, if desired. Place poached eggs in a bowl of cold water. Refrigerate if keeping more than a few hours. One hour before serving, replace cold water with very hot tap water. Repeat several times, until eggs are warmed through. When ready to use them, remove to dish towel to drain well.

RICH SHRIMP SAUCE

2 cups milk
4 tbs. butter
1/3 cup flour
1/2 tsp. salt
1/8 tsp. <u>each</u> white pepper and nutmeg
1/3 cup cream
1/3 lb. small cooked shrimp

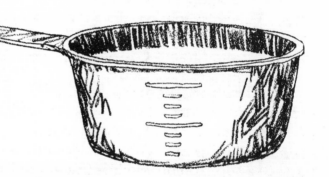

Heat milk to boiling. Melt butter in heavy saucepan. Stir in flour. Cook 2 minutes without browning. Remove from heat. Whisk in boiling milk. Add salt, pepper and nutmeg. Boil at least 3 minutes. (The French name for this mixture is bechamel). Cover bechamel with plastic pressed against the surface. About half an hour before serving time, stir cream and shrimp into bechamel. Transfer to the top of double boiler and heat over simmering water 20 to 30 minutes.

Filet of Beef Charlemagne

A most elegant presentation of roast filet of beef which can be assembled the day before. Very easy to serve since the filet is pre-sliced and requires no carving at serving time. Serve with bright green, barely cooked broccoli and Potato Puffs (page 114) or Creamy Potato Cheese Casserole (page 57).

2-1/2 to 3 lb. filet of beef
2 to 3 tbs. soft butter
salt and pepper
1 cup Duxelles* page 10
1-1/2 to 2 cups Tomato Herb Sauce, page 74
1-1/2 recipes Bearnaise Sauce, page 171

Trim filet of all surface fat and shiny outside skin which toughens when cooked. Tie every 1-1/2 inches around filet with string. Bring string lengthwise around under bottom and back to the first tie around the filet. This is to make the meat as uniform in shape as possible. Rub well with soft butter. Sprinkle all sides generously with salt and pepper. Place in small roasting pan. Roast uncovered in upper third of a 425°F oven

25 minutes. If possible baste once or twice with hot butter in roasting pan. Remove from oven and let cool. Remove string. Slice filet 1/4 to 3/8 inch thick. Lightly butter a 9 x 14-inch oval copper au gratin dish or similar type oven dish. Moisten duxelles with about half of tomato herb sauce. Reassemble slices of filet, keeping them in order, with a little tomato-duxelles mixture spread on each slice. Let slices tilt allowing some of the mixture to be visable between slices. (The reassembled filet will be a least one and a half times as long as the original.) Distribute any leftover duxelles mixture around the slices. Spoon remaining tomato herb sauce over reassembled slices. Cover lightly and refrigerate at this point, if desired. About 3 hours before serving, remove from refrigerator and let come to room temperature. This is important to the reheating time. Make Bearnaise sauce. Let sit, covered, at room temperature. About 1/2 hour before serving, cover filet with foil and reheat in 375°F oven. When thoroughly heated and just before serving, spoon Bearnaise sauce over top. Set under broiler, three inches from heat, to brown quickly. Makes 6 servings of a truly French dish.

*If preparing duxelles especially for this dish, use small mushrooms sliced with **slicing disc** rather than chopped, otherwise use what you have prepared.

Index

Albacore, Baked 51
Allumettes 120
Apple Crisp 48
Beef Filets In Flaky Pastry 122
Bouquet Garni 5
Bread
   Banana Squash 152
   Clarice's Brown 136
   Cinnamon Raisin-Nut 131
   Gingerbread 150
   Zucchini 60
Butter, Kneaded 8
Cake
   Carrot, Ollie's 61
   Cranberry 148
   Lemon Loaf 144
   Pound, Bourbon Nut 146
Carrot(s)
   Purée 86

   Raisin Salad 56
   With Herbs and Madeira 46
Cheese
   Cake, French 24
   Chopping and Shredding 15
   Cream, Whipped 40
   Fondue 54
   Ring, Puffy Swiss 110
   Ring, Roquefort 36
   Souffle 16
Chicken
   Breast Mousse 168
   Liver Pâté 77
   Livers, Sherried In Flaky Pastry 124
Cookies
   Crisp Butter-Nut 92
   French Butter Cookies 91
   Shortbread 90

Cream Puffs 107
   Small with Chocolate Sauce 108
Creme Calcutta 170
Cranberry Relish, Fresh 65
Crepes, Food Processor 156
Crepes, Stacked 159
Crumbs
   Bread 21
   Cookie 22
   Crusts 22
Cucumbers Vinaigrette 42
Danish Coffee Cake 139
Duxelles 10
Eggs
   Poached 175
   Poached, Ostendaise 174
   Stuffed, Mornay 12
Filet of Beef Charlemagne 178
Fish Fillets, Savory 70

Fish Patties 160
French Croutons 19
French Onion Soup 18
Fritters 115
Gingerbread 150
Ham Filled Crepes 158
Icing, Browned Butter 135
Icing, Vanilla Butter 149
Lemon Filling 100
Lemon Tartlettes 99
Lemon Zest 5
Lettuce, Braised 172
Mayonnaise 34
Mayonnaise, Mustard 35
Meat
   Chopping 26
   -Balls, Make-Ahead 68
   Loaf 28
Meringue 101

Mushroom(s)
Au Gratin 45
Marinated 44
Pâté, Merren's 66
Tartlettes 98
Pastry
Cream, French 109
For Tartelettes 96
Sweet Tart 99
Pastries, Flaky Sugar-Coated 121
Pâte à Choux 106
Peanut Butter, Spanish 14
Pecan Tartlettes 102
Persimmon Pudding, Carol's 87
Pie Crust, Easy-As 94
Pickle Slices, Fresh 43
Pizza 58
Pizza Crust 140
Poached Eggs Ostendaise 174

Potato(es)
Cheese Casserole, Creamy 57
Duchess 84
Gnocchi 112
Patties, Almond-Crusted 85
Puffs 114
Scalloped 47
Puff Paste, Quick 118
Puff Paste Tips 119
Quenelles of Sole 166
Roast Beef Hash Danish-Style 163
Rolls
Small Chocolate Filled 134
Crescent 130
Danish Sweet 132
Sauce
Apricot Rum 151
Bearnaise 171
Bordelaise 73

Brown 72
Cream 169
Dill 162
Hollandaise 52
Hungarian Paprika 75
Mornay 9
Mushroom 75
Pesto 71
Pizza 59
Rich Shrimp 177
Shrimp 167
Stroganoff 73
Sweet and Sour 29
Tomato Herb 74
Whiskey 63
Sausage, Country 30

Steak Tartare 27
Steamed Pudding,
  Grandma Thomason's 62
Swiss Delights 38
Swiss Steak A La Robert 49
Soup
  Cream of Celery 78
  Cream of Tomato 80
  Cream of Zucchini 79
  French Onion 18
  Pumpkin 82
Tomatoes, Broiled 23
Walnut Tartlettes 102
Yeast Dough, Rich 128
Yeast Loaves, Rich No-Knead 138

Thanks to Jackie, my students and friends who have shared their ideas and recipes. And, to my husband and children who have tolerated, encouraged and supported me in this venture.